INTERCESSORY PRAYER

INTERCESSORY PRAYER

edited by

Leonard LeSourd

HODDER AND STOUGHTON
LONDON SYDNEY AUCKLAND TORONTO

British Library Cataloguing in Publication Data

Intercessory prayer.
1. Christian Life. Prayer
I. LeSourd, Leonard E.
248.32

ISBN 0–340–53957–7

Published by Hodder and Stoughton, a division of Hodder and Stoughton Ltd, Mill Road, Dunton Green, Sevenoaks, Kent TN13 2YA. Editorial Office: 47 Bedford Square, London WC1B 3DP.

Printed in Great Britain by Cox & Wyman Ltd, Reading.

To:
Those intercessors who give
their time to an often lonely
but always fulfilling work

Contents

Introduction: How This Book Will Help You
Become an Effective Intercessor   15

I. When You Don't Know How to Pray   19

Portrait of an Intercessor
Betty Malz   21
Praying with Power for Others
Leonard LeSourd   24
Praying for Problems that Are Beyond Us
Richard Halverson   26
Why Answers Can Be Delayed
Catherine Marshall   30
When You Don't Want to Pray
Betsy Weight   34
Praying for Someone You Don't Like
John Sherrill   36

II. Praying for Those You Don't Know   41

When It's Someone You Don't Know
Leonard LeSourd   43
No One Had Ever Prayed for Them
Jamie Buckingham   46
When Prayer Comes Alive
Theresa Mulligan   50
Praying for that Unborn Child
Ed Corley   53
Another Way to Pray
John Sherrill   55

III. Learning to Listen   57

How I Learned to Hear God's Voice
Mark Virkler   59

Contents

What Is God Saying to You?
Leonard LeSourd 63

IV. Overcoming Obstacles in Your Prayer Life . . . 69

A Fast on Criticalness
Catherine Marshall 71
The Cost of Unforgiveness
Charles C. Carrin 74
Working Through the Dry Period
Betsy Weight 77
The Problem with Pride
David Wilkerson 80
When Prayer Is Manipulation
Germaine Copeland 83
When You Feel Far from God
Sondra Johnson 86

V. Combat in the Heavenlies 89

The Daily Call to Spiritual Warfare
Leonard LeSourd 91
Extra Power in a Crisis
Jean Ware 95
When We Are Called to Battle
David Hazard 98
Can Our Prayers Change God's Mind?
Brother Andrew 101
Let the Lord Fight for You
H. David Edwards 104
When Temptation Overwhelms You
Catherine Marshall 107
A Warrior's Prayer
Victor M. Matthews 111
Esther: A Courageous Lady
Derek Prince 113

VI. Scriptural Praying 117

How Scripture Strengthens Personal Prayer
Edith Marshall 119

Contents

What Can Happen When You Pray God's Word
Leonard LeSourd 123
Jesus, Our Intercessor
Sondra Johnson 126
The Penny Prayer
Elizabeth Sherrill 129

VII. Igniting the Church 133

Love on Its Knees
Dick Eastman 135
How God Dealt with a Successful
(But Complacent) Church
Jim Croft 140
The Need for Watering Holes
Margaret Therkelsen 145
A New Kind of Prayer Meeting
Jack W. Hayford 148

VIII. Going Deeper 153

The Cost of Intercession
Colleen Townsend Evans 155
Persistence in Prayer
George R. Callahan 159
Prophetic Intercession
Nancy Oliver LeSourd 163
Earning that "Gained Position"
Norman Grubb 167
The Mercy Prayer
Catherine Marshall 170
Why Intercessors Fast
Leonard LeSourd 174
Travailing Prayer
June G. Coxhead 177

IX. In Search of a Miracle 181

The Soaking Prayer
Francis MacNutt 183

Contents

Faith as a Little Child
Virginia Lively 187

Split-Second Prayer
Don V. Bovey 190

Wanted! . . . for the Lord
Sandra Simpson LeSourd 193

The Right Prayer at the Right Time
Joseph P. Bishop 197

The Astonishing Power of One Mother's Prayers
Sondra Johnson 200

Rees Howells: Catalyst for a Miracle
Leonard LeSourd 204

Why Are We Afraid to Believe in Miracles?
Lloyd J. Ogilvie 207

X. Angelic Protection 211

Angels Watching Over You and Me
Betty Malz 213

God's Special Helpers
Leonard LeSourd 216

On a Road in the Middle East
Deborah Strong 222

XI. Intercessors in Action 225

Emergency Prayer
Peggy Sparks 227

Intercessor at Work
Nate Larkin 229

Standing in the Gap for Coalinga
Richard Schneider 231

Burden for Our Nation's Capital
Barbara Melin 234

When Your Flight Is Canceled
B. J. Funk 237

Three Miles with the Lord
Leonard LeSourd 240

Contents

An Orchid for Mary
   Sandra Simpson LeSourd 243

XII. God at Work in Our Lives 247

Introduction

How This Book Will Help You Become an Effective Intercessor

First a challenge: You should be an intercessor if you are not one already!

Why?

Because you will touch God's heart when you pray for other people. *Touching the Heart of God on Behalf of Others* will help you become an effective intercessor because it is built upon the basic elements of years of teaching provided by the Breakthrough newsletter.

The Breakthrough ministry was established by my late wife, Catherine Marshall, and myself as a nonprofit book outreach to prisoners and missionaries. It was expanded in the spring of 1980 to include the work of intercession when Catherine was given a vision of a new work.

Weighed heavily with the acute needs of many people, a large portion coming to her through the mail, Catherine began to pray for wisdom in answering them. As she did, a vision began to take shape in her mind. It was composed of two parts.

She described it this way: "One part was a huge group of people—wounded, thirsty, frightened sheep who had lost their way and were reaching out, asking frantically for help. The second was a growing number of Christians—the retired, the handicapped, those with the time and desire to do something for others. In letters I receive from these, they are forever asking, 'How can I make my life really count for something? I'd like to serve Jesus in some way, but I'm so limited in movement.' "

In the vision Catherine saw the two parts—need and supply—coming together through some central coordinating effort. On the one hand, those asking for prayer, the lonely and isolated, the ones desperate to know that Jesus loved them. On the other hand, the retired, the bored, the handicapped, those with time on their hands—time to care, to write letters, to pray. And the work meeting the needs on both sides was the work of intercession.

Catherine soon began to realize that intercessory prayer is the most important work there is in the Kingdom. "In fact," she said, "so important that the Pioneer and Captain of our salvation, Jesus Christ Himself, 'ever liveth to make intercession' for us" (Hebrews 7:25, KJV).

She also knew that intercession meant work—time and dedication—for those who would agree to devote themselves to making the vision a reality.

It further meant coordinating communications with the intercessors, not only to send the prayer requests to them, but to offer teaching and discoveries and insights and encouragement.

Before long the dream was a reality. The work of "The Intercessors" was underway.

Catherine wrote a short article for *Charisma* magazine asking, "Would you like to be a part of a new intercessory prayer work?" In a few months we had five hundred intercessors at work.

We prayed for people to come who could coordinate the inflow and outflow of communications. God sent them. He touched the hearts of those He wanted to give to the work.

And we began the Breakthrough newsletter, with articles and insights by veteran intercessors as well as those just discovering the joyous work of intercession.

It is from the decade of teaching—and learning from "The Intercessors"—that this book has developed. If you are a new intercessor, you might consider this book as a training manual. If you are a veteran prayer warrior, I suggest you use this book as a refresher course.

Don't try to read it all in one sitting. Instead, include it as a part of your devotions. Refer to it when you need encouragement or when your faith is faltering. Look through the table of contents for the section that especially relates to where you are today.

If you are involved in spiritual warfare, for instance, turn to that section.

If you are going through a dry period, find teaching on that subject in the section "Overcoming Obstacles."

Perhaps you would like to begin an intercession program in your church. Insights by pastors Jim Croft and Jack Hayford can help you there.

You might be seeking an understanding of travail, prophetic intercession, the "gained position," praying in the Spirit; you can find answers in the section "Going Deeper."

Or if you need assurance that God is a God of miracles, turn to the section on that important subject.

The people writing segments for this book include such outstanding leaders as Lloyd Ogilvie, Senate Chaplain Richard Halverson, Betty Malz, Derek Prince, Colleen Evans, John and Elizabeth Sherrill, Jamie Buckingham, Francis MacNutt, David Wilkerson and many others.

Yet the cornerstone of this work is the multitude of little-known people in small towns in America and throughout the world. These faithful, tenacious prayer warriors are the real giants of intercession. It is to them we dedicate this book.

If you would like to become involved, there are three things you can do:

1. If you are not an intercessor and would like to become one simply write to: Breakthrough, Lincoln, Virginia 22078, c/o New Intercessor Department, and ask for the information sheet.

2. If you would like to receive the newsletter at no cost to

you, write and ask for it at the same address as above, care of *The Breakthrough Intercessor*.

3. If you have a prayer concern for yourself or for someone close to you, send it to the same address, care of Prayer Need, Breakthrough, Lincoln, Virginia 22078.

Our prayer is that you will not only use this book as a guideline for yourself and your family, but will also heed God's call for more and more intercessors by sharing its message with others and encouraging them to become involved. For as Catherine expressed it when the Lord gave her the vision of the work ahead: "He made it oh, so clear: Intercession is where the action will be for a long, long time."

May God bless you.

Leonard LeSourd and
The Breakthrough Staff

I
When You Don't Know How to Pray

As an intercessor, you begin by an open and frank admission: "I am not qualified to be an intercessor if being one is dependent on my own strength and skills. I will never know enough to be a prayer warrior. It can happen only as God is my strength . . . only as His Spirit gives me the perception and the tenacity and the wisdom to pray effectively for others."

This section portrays a powerful prayer warrior in action, lays out the basics in prayer work and, through the experiences of people like Senate Chaplain Richard Halverson, John Sherrill, Catherine Marshall and Betsy Weight, explains how one "gets out of the way" so that the Holy Spirit can take over.

Portrait of an Intercessor

Betty Malz

Author of *My Glimpse of Eternity*
and other books; from Crystal
Beach, Florida.

My first encounter with an all-out "prayer warrior" came
when I was at a young, impressionable age. My Uncle Cecil, a
World War II pilot, was seriously injured when he crash-landed
his plane in England. The moment the cablegram arrived, I
heard my parents say, "Let's call Old Warhorse Buckland!" The
call was placed to a location several hundred miles away.

Two days later we got word that Uncle Cecil had regained
consciousness and would recover. He went on to make a career
in the Air Force, is now retired and serves on the advisory
board of Douglas Aircraft.

Months later a distraught woman knocked on the door of our
house late one night. When my father opened the door she
sobbed, "Ralph has gone wild again, Pastor. Please call the
police."

Instead of calling the police my dad put on his overcoat and
barked an order to Mother, "Call Old Warhorse Buckland!"

I don't know what happened other than that my father coun-
seled the woman and her demented husband—and that "Old
Warhorse Buckland" prayed. Two Sundays later Ralph came to

the altar after church and accepted Jesus as his personal Savior. In the years that followed he became a loving husband and a responsible parent.

What a powerhouse the Old Warhorse must be! I thought. The day finally came when Old Warhorse Buckland was coming for dinner. We children (I was about ten) could hardly wait. I envisioned him as a seven-foot giant of a man with booming voice and flashing eyes, who might even ride to our house on a large white horse.

Old Warhorse arrived in a small car. Dad hurried down to the street to help *her* out of the backseat, and she tottered up the porch steps. She was small-boned, small in size and plainly dressed.

I was terribly let down until I looked into her face. Gray hair; firm, resolute chin; patrician nose; character lines creasing her forehead like rivulets. But it was her eyes that held me. They flashed determination, tenacity, power. Flecks of fire seemed to emanate from the gray irises of her eyes.

I trembled when she took my hand, but her voice was gentle. She so inspired my confidence that I asked her how she got her prayer power.

Out came the story of her life. As a girl she was plain; she could not sing, play an instrument or even sew very well. She was too small for sports. But she did love to read.

Stories of courage fascinated her. She fantasized about riding horses to battle. As an American Joan of Arc, she vanquished the forces of evil in every skirmish. When she became an all-out believer, she transferred her battles to the spiritual realm. And then came the discovery: God had given her the gift of prayer power for others!

The label *Old Warhorse* came afterward. She rode horses to battle figuratively as she fought the forces of Satan. Her prayers were not loud; they were intense, prolonged—in fact, unceasing. As she prayed for people in crisis, she put on the whole armor of God, claimed the power of Jesus, mounted her horse and went against "the rulers, against the authorities, against the powers of this dark world and against the spiritual forces of evil in the heavenly realms" (Ephesians 6:12, NIV).

Old Warhorse didn't need to leave her house to wage her battles. When Uncle Cecil was near death, she called upon ministering angels to come to his aid even though he was thousands of miles away in a foreign hospital. The demons that possessed Ralph did not have a chance against Old Warhorse. She took authority, called for warrior angels and Ralph was delivered.

This "little" woman did not stop her prayer when the enemy was in retreat. She kept praying after the victory was won, only too aware that the enemy would return if given a chance. Too many victories have turned into defeats, she maintained, because the celebrating people let down their defenses.

But great battles have also been won and lives changed because Old Warhorse and people like her believed in the power of prayer and were willing to put it into action.

Praying with Power for Others

Leonard LeSourd

Chairman of Breakthrough; former editor, *Guideposts* magazine; associate publisher, Chosen Books; from Lincoln, Virginia

Not many intercessors have the power of "Old Warhorse Buckland," especially beginners. For those starting out in this prayer work, here are some guidelines for basic training.

1. Set aside *a specific time* or several times each day, if possible, to pray.
2. *One specific place* for prayer is the ideal, but it is not essential.
3. *Prepare* by quieting your heart and mind. It helps to reread some of the great Scripture passages on intercession (such as Isaiah 59:16; Romans 8:26–39; Ephesians 1:17–23; Hebrews 2:8–18; Hebrews 7:14–28).
4. See the person for whom you are praying as being *in the presence of Jesus* with His light shining around and through that person, penetrating every cell of that person's body. See the person as Jesus does. If emotions need healing, see them as becoming stable; if there are body ailments, see them as becoming whole. Remember that where Jesus is, there is Light; darkness, sickness of mind or spirit or body,

24

distorted and broken relationships—all these must be dissolved by His Light or flee.

5. *Be objective* about the person and the problem. Clear away all emotional underbrush. Do not be misled into thinking that your emotional involvement is necessary or even desirable. God's power is what matters, not our feelings. Our sense of weakness can be His strength.

6. *Listen.* God speaks to us most often by planting a thought in our minds. Do not be discouraged if nothing comes through right away. Keep listening. Keep asking for His ideas, His help, His guidance.

7. *Write down* what you hear. Do not try to evaluate or interpret what you think God might be saying about the person you are praying for. If over a period of a week or more you continue to get the same message about any person you are praying for, ask God for guidance about passing His word along to that person.

8. Peace and joy in your spirit are often given you as the sign that the prayer is being answered.

Praying for Problems that Are Beyond Us

Richard Halverson

Chaplain, United States Senate;
from Washington, D.C.

During the eight years that I have been chaplain of the United States Senate here in Washington, D.C., I have become increasingly aware of one basic fact: *The deepest problems of this world are mostly beyond man's ability to find a solution.*

This is not a statement of despair and hopelessness. I believe there are solutions—but they will not come through man's skills. They will come through God's mercy and wisdom.

If you resist this premise, I understand. Most of us, especially politicians, do not like being in a position of helplessness.

Yet Scripture contains many hard truths in this area that have stood the test of time. Here's a verse in Romans, for example, that is very unpopular in our culture. Folks do not want to hear it:

> For the creation was subjected to frustration, not by its own choice, but by the will of the one who subjected it, in hope. . . .
>
> Romans 8:20, NIV

Now it seems to me that we're beginning to see a subliminal sense of frustration everywhere. Our government officials, for example, can't even deal with the national debt or balance the budget for one year, let alone deal with the drug problem.

Through this passage in Romans Paul is telling us that God in His sovereign purpose submitted human history to frustration! That's why we're never satisfied. Then comes this verse: "We know that the whole creation has been groaning as in the pains of childbirth. . . ."

We have here a picture of a woman in the delivery room groaning to bring forth a child. And Paul says that this is the condition of the whole created universe. All of the troubles we see in the world everywhere, whether in the Middle East or Central America or wherever—all these troubles are the whole created universe in the delivery room groaning for deliverance.

I would like for us to look at it this way: *We are not seeing the death rattle of a civilization; we're seeing the birth pangs of a new creation!*

Then we come to the words (verse 26) that so many of us struggle with: "In the same way, the Spirit helps us in our weakness. We do not know what we ought to pray for, but the Spirit himself intercedes for us with groans that words cannot express."

It is my profound conviction that *we are really not praying in the Spirit until we go beyond the ability to verbalize.* As long as we can verbalize prayers, we're always subject to our own ideas, our own hopes, our own dreams, our own ambitions, our own aspirations. But when we just groan inwardly, because we don't know how to ask or even what to ask for, then God can take over. In the last eight years I have resorted to this passage in Romans again and again because I honestly do not know how to pray for some of these things that I'm so much aware of.

When I go into the Senate Chamber, I listen to the debate as much as I can. I spend as much time on the floor as possible and thus am privy to the problems of the whole world.

One senator, for example, is deeply concerned that we are destroying our environment. Consider the problem of garbage, one of the biggest concerns we have in America today. What to do with waste? Especially the paper product that is harder than metal to tear. Just think of the amount of non-biodegradable material—millions of tons of it—that we manufacture and then dump in the ocean. It will never dissolve. We can't get rid of it. And we call that progress.

I have lunch occasionally with a man in the Department of Energy whose sole responsibility is to find a way to get rid of nuclear wastes. At times it is difficult to be with him because he represents such an incredible burden. No states want nuclear waste dumped in their areas. So all over the nation we keep it in storehouses. We don't know what to do with them. And we call nuclear power progress.

How do you pray about those things?

Or take the national debt. Now I'm not an economist. I have difficulty balancing my own checkbook. But every day I hear from someone how many billions of dollars we spend just paying the interest on the national debt.

The other day at lunch I listened to discussions about how much wealth Japan has accumulated, how much land it owns in the United States. One man there who knows, said, "If the Japanese should liquidate their relatively small island, their property is so expensive they'd have enough money to buy all of the United States of America—twice over!"

At a reception last week someone said that every thirty seconds in the United States a teenager attempts suicide. I couldn't believe it. So at a luncheon the next day with four senators, I passed on this fact. They couldn't believe it either. One senator went to his desk later and checked it out. "It's correct," he told me. *Every thirty seconds in the United States a teenager attempts suicide.*

How do you pray about these things?

There are a million children on the streets of our cities selling their bodies to get drugs. Many of them are very young girls and boys. And in 68% of such cases when the authorities find the families of those children and contact them, the parent or person in charge says, "You keep them. We don't want them." How do you pray about that?

I feel deeply about these problems. I also feel frustration and futility. There's nothing I can do, except pray, and so often I don't know how to pray.

It is then I remember those verses in Romans; Paul says this was his experience, too. So I accept my groaning as the Spirit of God within me praying.

This encourages me to believe I'm allowing my own body to be a groaning ground for God so that He can use my helplessness to accomplish His purposes for us.

Why Answers Can Be Delayed

Catherine Marshall

Founder of Breakthrough; author of fifteen books including *A Man Called Peter* and *Christy*

A friend tells me, "For eight years I've been praying that my son John, now married and with three children, will become God's man. I know that what I'm asking is His will. And John's three children need a Christian father. So—why such a long-delayed answer to prayer?"

Another friend writes me, "Ted's affair with that 'other woman' still goes on. I love my husband and this is devastating to our teenagers. I've prayed every way I know to pray. My spiritual skies are leaden. God doesn't seem to hear me. Help!"

Is there in your life a cherished heart's desire taken to God over and over in prayer, yet still unfulfilled? Then link hands with my two friends, and with the rest of us, and with all prayer warriors across the centuries! No wonder Jesus had so much to say about persistence in prayer, along with His clear teaching that sometimes we will have to wait for God to move, thus the requirement of patience on our side (Matthew 7:7–11; Matthew 15:22–28; Luke 11:5–10).

And Jesus' actions were always consistent with His teaching. In the miracle of raising from the dead His friend Lazarus, Jesus acted out His teaching on the necessity of our persistence in prayer and the patience needed in a situation in which the answer was so slow as to seem too late.

The drama of this occurs in the eleventh chapter of John. The first few verses set the scene . . . Lazarus' home in the village of Bethany, less than two miles from Jerusalem. It was the Master's favorite retreat spot, where He could relax with His friends—Martha and Mary, the two sisters, and Lazarus—who were dear to Him.

The sisters had sent an urgent message to the Master. "Lord, he whom you love so much is desperately ill. Please come quickly."

One morning in rereading this story, the transition word between verses 5 and 6 was not only underscored, it all but leapt off the page:

"Jesus loved Martha and her sister and Lazarus; [they were His dear friends . . . *Therefore*, [even] when He heard that Lazarus was sick, He still stayed two days longer in the same place where He was" (TAB). And Lazarus died!

Verse 5: He loved this little family especially.

Verse 6: *Therefore* He delayed going to them in their distress. How odd! Why?

Martha and Mary did not understand either. Separately, each sister verbalized the same thought, "Lord, if You had been here, our brother would not have died. You could have prevented it."

Distressed by their grief to the point of tears (verse 35), Jesus gave two reasons for His deliberate delay: First, this experience was going to increase their faith, that is, their ability to trust Him in the midst of seemingly impossible circumstances (verse 15); and second, they were to have an even greater firsthand demonstration of the glory of God (verse 40).

In reading again the Lazarus story, the Spirit would give you the same message He gave to me . . . Jesus loves you especially. You are His special friend. *Therefore* He delays. The *therefore* has wrapped in it the limitless love of God, with Jesus experiencing to the full, along with us, our concern, agony of spirit and sorrow.

Meanwhile, where do we get the needed patience? When the situation shows no change or even grows worse (as in the Lazarus account), how do we hang on to the faith that God's love *is* working out our problems?

Marge, a dear friend of mine, shared an experience in which the Lord spoke to her directly about the "how." She and her husband had just learned that he had Parkinson's disease. It was the sort of dread disease Marge had always especially feared.

The entire family gathered, anointed their father and husband with oil, asked the Lord for His healing, then made a deliberate act of turning the situation over to Him.

Marge's heart questioned, "Until such time as our family sees this prayer answered, how can I keep enough peace of mind not to let worry and fear impede or stop my daily work?"

God answered her question directly in an experience Marge had aboard a plane bound for Cleveland, waiting for take-off. . . .

As she settled into her seat, Marge noticed a strange phenomenon. On one side of the airplane a sunset suffused the entire sky with glorious color. But out of the window next to her seat all Marge could see was a sky dark and threatening, with no sign of the sunset.

The plane's engines began to roar, and a closed-in feeling came over Marge. Long since, she had learned at such moments to be still and listen within. Then the gentle Voice spoke, *You have noticed the windows,* He said, even in the roar and thrust of the takeoff. *For a while now your life will contain some happy, beautiful times, but also some dark shadows.*

Here's a lesson I want to teach you to save you much heartache and allow you to "abide in Me" with continual peace and joy. . . . You see, it doesn't matter which window you look through, this plane is still going to Cleveland.

So it is in your life. You have a choice. You can dwell on the gloomy picture. Or you can focus on the bright things in your life and leave the dark, ominous situations to Me. I alone can handle the dark ones anyway. And the final destination is not influenced by what you see or feel along the way.

Learn this, act on it and you will be released, able to experience the "peace that passes understanding," even My joy.

Marge's sharing is helping me to handle my "meanwhiles." Not one of us finds it easy to put our problems into His hands that completely. But only in that way can our trust in Him grow and our prayer life mature.

When You Don't Want to Pray

Betsy Weight

Prayer warrior and freelance
writer; from Eskdale, Utah

All of us go through low periods when we simply do not feel like praying. When this happened to me not too long ago, God enlisted me in a program based on His knowledge of a deep desire I had to play the flute. By opening the way for me to pursue that desire, He drew me into an adventure in prayer consistent with the unsearchable riches of His love.

Only God knows why He waited until I entered the fourth decade of life, but that was the time He let an old flute fall into my hands and stirred a mysterious and demanding drive to learn it. I cannot say at what point I realized He had allowed me to have the flute in order to draw me into prayer, but I came to know, without a doubt, that the entire learning process was to be applied to prayer—and that prayer was the principal thing.

When we listen to the Holy Spirit, He will use our everyday experiences to give us insight and understanding on the invisible realm of our walk of faith. Many times I did not want to practice. The reasons were as many and as varied as those I found for not wanting to pray, but I soon learned that to achieve success in either, I required daily commitment to "practice"—

whether I felt like it or not. The result of daily, disciplined practice was clearly evident in my increasing ability to get sound out of the flute. As the beauty of the music increased, I was asking the Lord to show me how to relate the same principles to prayer. As I practiced scales to build a foundation for music, I asked to see what was needed to build a solid foundation for prayer and a closer walk with Him.

The key word was always *practice*. "Practice what you have learned" (Philippians 4:9, TAB). Where scales are the foundation for freedom in performing music, knowing the Word of God is the foundation for freedom to move in prayer as directed by the Holy Spirit. As the music became more difficult, I always found it required faith to believe I could accomplish it and practice to achieve it. When the foundation is firm there is a rest in knowing it is there; however, climbing to new heights will always require that basic faith, coupled with perseverance, to attain the goal. As I yielded to cleansing in my life and His Spirit found in me an increasingly clear "instrument" for prayer, He correspondingly provided me with finer flutes that would respond to greater expression in music (Hebrews 11:6).

Watch an accomplished musician. Through years of disciplined training, music has become part of his being. He no longer thinks of scales, theory or composition; there is a dynamic flow of harmony within him and he lives and breathes music. So, too, with prayer. Study the life of someone who has learned to "dwell in the secret place of the Most High" (Psalm 91:1, TAB). He no longer thinks separately of praise, thanksgiving or sacrifice—he lives it and to pray is as natural as to breathe.

Pray because God desires and commands it (Matthew 7:7–8). Do not be surprised when He blesses you "exceeding abundantly above all that we ask or think" (Ephesians 3:20, KJV). In fact, for His glory, expect it!

Praying for Someone You Don't Like

John Sherrill

Author of *My Friend, the Bible*;
co-author of many books including *The Cross and the
Switchblade*; from Westchester
County, New York

Our telephone rang one evening with news that a member of
our church was filing papers for bankruptcy. Apparently Art
was taking his business failure pretty hard. "You know how
depressed Art can get," the man on the phone was saying.
"Hope you'll pray."

Of course I said I'd pray. I meant it, too. We have an informal
intercessory prayer chain at church, which we take seriously.

Which made it all the more difficult for me, then, when I
found I had trouble keeping my promise. As soon as I began
to pray for Art (I have, of course, changed both his name and
the situation he faced) my mind wandered into business
problems of my own. I tried to force my attention back but
the effort backfired. All I recalled was a condescending stout
little man who had a way of making me mad. Art once tried
to get the church to elect only Republicans to the vestry because all Democrats were "bleeding heart pinkos, if not Fellow Travelers." He poked me in the ribs when he said this,
but he wasn't laughing. "Present company excepted, old
man," he allowed.

36

The trouble was that I was being asked to pray for a man I just did not like.

This created a peculiar problem for me as it often does, no doubt, for anyone interested in intercession. Up until that prayer request I could handle my dislike for Art by simply keeping my distance. If I saw him coming in one door I slipped out the other, feeling guilty at my timidness but avoiding him nonetheless.

Suddenly, now, I could no longer run away. I was in a bind; I could not pray effectively for Art, but because of my commitment I could not avoid thinking about him either.

In the middle of this struggle, my wife, Tib, and I had Sunday brunch with a new friend from church, a remarkable woman who gave me a brace of tools for dealing with the dilemma of how to pray for someone you don't like.

As we stood in line at the Holiday Inn buffet we learned that Sylvia Harmon had lost her young husband when their children were two and four years old. Armed with a degree as a Registered Nurse, Sylvia saw her daughter through Columbia Medical School and is watching with satisfaction as her son completes his graduate work in architecture at Harvard.

It was Sylvia's experience as an R.N. that turned out to be so helpful to me. We had begun to talk about nursing and I asked Sylvia what she found to be the hardest part of her profession. "That's easy," she said. "It's that sometimes you have to nurse people you don't like."

I was all attention. I told Sylvia about the similar problem I faced in intercessory prayer. "It's difficult," I said, "to pray for people who are very off-putting."

"I know," said Sylvia. "And the trouble is you feel guilty because we're supposed to pray for spiteful people."

As we ate, Sylvia told Tib and me two examples, from her own career, of people who had used her despitefully. She once had a lawyer patient who had been shot in the head and who afterward suffered a personality change. He would shout obscenities at the nurses. "I felt dirty when I walked out of that man's room," Sylvia said.

"And there was a woman I once nursed on private duty,"

she went on to say, finishing her eggs Benedict. "She had melanoma. In a few weeks she would probably be dead and yet she wanted to be sure she got her money's worth out of us nurses. She couldn't bear to see me sit down. I had to be in motion for eight hours. If I so much as slowed my pace she was asking for a Kleenex or a cup of tea."

The question, of course, was what to do? How did Sylvia manage the problem in her most-intercesssory of professions, nursing?

There were two principles, Sylvia said, that had helped her.

First, when she was still a student at the School of Nursing at Howard University, she had been trained to be impartial. "We were taught," she said, "to treat all patients with the same caring." Impartiality. That is the way God treats us. *He causes his sun to rise on the evil and the good, and sends rain on the righteous and the unrighteous* (Matthew 5:45, NIV).

"The second principle is harder," said Sylvia, "but it is even more helpful. I must remember that I am here to nurse, not to judge." Again this principle is based on the way God treats us. My mind raced over a statement from Jesus (which I had to wait till I got home to be able to quote correctly). *The Father judges no one, but has entrusted all judgment to the Son* (John 5:22, NIV).

"There's a bonus that comes from using these two yard-sticks," Sylvia said as I paid the bill. "Once you stop judging you are free to understand. How much truth there is in the old cliché that to understand all is to forgive all. The lawyer who shouted at me knew he'd never again be clear of mind. I'd rail, too, wouldn't you? And the woman dying of cancer: She had no belief in an afterlife. She was saying she wanted to live and hoped she would continue to need her money."

After our brunch with Sylvia Harmon, I once again thought about Art and his business crisis and I felt ashamed of my judgmentalism. We can be realistic and clear-eyed about personality weaknesses, yes. But to *judge* to the point where we cannot intercede? Even the Father did not do that. He left judgment to the Son and the reason seems clear: Jesus Himself walked through the rejections and temptations of life and could identify with our weaknesses.

He had been there. He knew. To understand all is to forgive all. Within moments I found that I was able to begin a fresh kind of intercession for Art, trusting at the same time that when others interceded for *me* they could find it in themselves not to judge me first.

II
Praying for Those You Don't Know

You may occasionally be asked by friends to pray for someone you have never met. How do you accomplish this?

Following are a number of ideas used successfully by other intercessors. Though the methods may vary, this is one opportunity you will not want to miss! It may even be that we can minister most effectively to strangers, since we are freed from the limitations of our personal views and must rely on God to direct our prayers.

When It's Someone You Don't Know

Leonard LeSourd

Chairman of Breakthrough; former editor, *Guideposts* magazine; associate publisher, Chosen Books; from Lincoln, Virginia

The three names on my list—Fred, Susan and Emily—soon became quite familiar to me, as did their problems. As part of the Breakthrough intercessory prayer program, I prayed for them early each morning for three weeks. When their names came to mind during the day—while in the car, walking, watching the news on TV—I would pray for them again.

To share my thoughts on praying for someone you don't know, I'm going to focus on only one name—Fred. Here is the synopsis I was given of his need.

> Fred is a homosexual, but says he doesn't want to be. He wants to give his life to God and be what God wants him to be. Yet each time he makes progress, something holds him back and he slips again into his sin. He has thoughts of suicide and seeks prayer help to be free from his bondage.

First, since I didn't know Fred, I asked the Lord to make him more real to me. It was important to me to develop a picture of

Fred. Bit by bit his characteristics began to emerge . . . a young-ish, single man, tenderhearted, confused and frustrated. I sensed his heart-hunger for God, a longing for the loving father figure perhaps he never had.

Since the prayer request came from a woman who said she was a friend of Fred, I guessed that Fred had a capacity for friendship. "Thank you, Lord, for this friend who cared enough to ask for prayer for him. Bless and protect her."

Next, before I could pray for Fred I knew I had to be free of judgment of him. What were my feelings toward homosexuals?

Sadness for one. Their choice of this lifestyle rules out so many joys—for example, being husband and father—unless they are bisexuals. And there is no way I could conceive of an active bisexual becoming a good husband and father.

Anger, too. Years ago the thought of homosexuals even try-ing to corrupt my children made me livid. I resented their attempts to be recognized as having a normal, acceptable life-style when God's Word thundered that this was sinful living. Leviticus 20:13, for example, states: "If a man lies with a male as with a woman, both of them have committed an abomina-tion" (RSV).

But Fred wanted to be free. I could rejoice in that. The Spirit of God was already at work in him. Others were praying for him, too. "Lord, I feel free of any judgment toward Fred. I pray for his complete healing."

Now to come against the strongholds that were keeping Fred in bondage. At some point an unnatural desire had entered Fred. I prayed that Fred would renounce this unholy desire to lust, repent of his behavior, seek God's forgiveness.

Then I recognized another stronghold keeping Fred in bondage—suicide thoughts. The enemy in control of Fred was a seducer, a deceiver and a destroyer, "I come against this suicide spirit in Fred in the name of Jesus," I prayed.

One day as I interceded I sensed there was much fear in Fred. AIDS. Another stronghold to attack.

Reports from prayer warriors agree on one point. Freeing homosexuals from bondage calls for the most intensive kind of spiritual warfare. But in Fred's synopsis were these heartening words: "He wants to give his life to God and be what God wants him to be." Though it was necessary to come against the strongholds of lust, of suicide thoughts and of fear in Fred, how important also for me to stress the positive in my prayer. "Lord, thank You for this major step by Fred toward the light. Reach down and touch Fred in a supernatural way as You did with St. Paul on the Damascus Road."

Then came this revelation: The Lord loved Fred. He was pouring down His love for this emotionally mixed-up man. Fred was being bathed in God's love and forgiveness.

"Thank You, Lord, for the way You hate the sin but love the sinner. Thank You, too, for the reminder of 1 Corinthians 6:19–20: 'Do you not know that your body is the temple of the Holy Spirit who is in you, whom you have from God, and you are not your own? For you were bought at a price; therefore glorify God in your body and in your spirit, which are God's' " (NKJV).

No One Had Ever Prayed for Them

Jamie Buckingham

Editor-in-chief, *Ministries Today* magazine; pastor, Tabernacle Church; from Melbourne, Florida

I've been stretched by a fascinating prayer assignment recently—to pray for a tiny village of unbelievers deep in the New Guinea jungle. It came about this way.

At the request of Wycliffe Bible Translators, I flew from my home town of Melbourne, Florida, last summer to speak to their Indonesian branch at Irian Jaya in western New Guinea. The final part of the journey was a 200-mile flight in a single engine plane over impenetrable jungle to a tiny airstrip, hacked out of the trees, where the missionary compound is located.

While at the mission compound, I read a survey report submitted by a team of translators, who had just discovered a never-before-known tribe of people deep in the heart of the Indonesian jungle. These tribal people—who called themselves "Doa"—live on a small river hundreds of miles from the mission compound where I was staying.

A pilot had spotted their tiny village one day while flying over an uncharted section of the jungle. He had reported the discovery to Dr. Dick Hugoniot, the director of the Indonesian branch of Wycliffe. Dick, in turn, had sent out two men to see if they could reach this unknown tribe. The survey team had traveled several days in a dugout canoe up a small jungle river. When the river became impassable because of rocks and logs, they carried their canoe through the snake-infested jungle until they could put it back into the water. It took almost two weeks of traveling and searching before they found the tribal village.

The Doa people, they learned, had no alphabet, no written language, and had never been exposed to the outside world. Their entire tribal population was fewer than 300—and only two of them had ever seen a white man before. They stayed alive by hunting with bows and arrows, and fishing in the river.

Tragically, they had never heard about God, much less about His Son, Jesus.

"When will it be possible to send a translation team to the Doa people?" I asked Dick Hugoniot.

"It will be years," he said. "There are more than two hundred tribes in Indonesia, all of whom speak different languages. We have workers in only seventeen of those. The Doa people will just have to wait.

When I returned to the States I couldn't shake my burden for these 300 individuals who lived in such spiritual darkness. I had never met any of them. I hadn't even seen where they lived. But the "burden" was on my heart to pray for them—to intercede on their behalf.

I wrote Wycliffe headquarters in Huntington Beach, California, to ask if anyone was praying on a regular basis for the Doas. A Wycliffe worker wrote back that no one was praying for the Doas. She sent me a little card, which I taped over my desk, that read: "I am praying daily for the Doa people of Irian Jaya until they have God's Word in their own language." It was accompanied by a verse, Psalm 65:2, "O thou that hearest prayer, unto thee shall all flesh come" (KJV).

I confess, I was both excited and frightened over this commitment. I had never prayed for a tribe of people—especially people I didn't know. Then there was the factor of *daily* prayer. Could I discipline myself to pray for them *every* day? The card was taped right beside my word processor where I go to work each morning. It takes about thirty seconds, after I turn on the machine, to "boot up"—that is, to load my program into the computer. Normally that is "dead" time. I just sit there each morning while my disk drive whirrs and whines—waiting for the screen to light up and indicate it is ready for me to go to work. I decided to use those thirty seconds to pray for the Doas.

But something happened. Each morning, as I prayed during that "boot up" time, I began to receive little "visions." I could picture those little grass huts on the sandbar along the river. In my mind's eye, I could see the brown-skinned people wandering around the tiny village. Children were playing along the river. Women were working with the materials their men brought in from the jungle. Men, with their bows and long arrows, were roaming the jungle or paddling their dugout canoes in search of food.

Then I saw them afraid at night—afraid of demons, afraid of the snakes and crocodiles, afraid of the dark. I could see the witch doctor trying to use his power to hold back the spiritual darkness. Often my thirty-second prayer time went to five, sometimes ten minutes. On several occasions, I actually began to cry as I prayed for those unknown people—lost and without hope.

I asked God to send a Bible translator who would learn their language, translate the Bible and teach them to read the Word of God.

Six months later, I was in California to speak to the combined boards of Wycliffe. During one of my sessions, I mentioned I was praying for the Doa people.

At the close of that session, a man from Indonesia came forward. He was excited. "Just last week," he said, "Peter and Mary Jane Munnings, Wycliffe members from Canada now living in Irian Jaya, entered the Doa village as translators. They were years ahead of schedule, but when the word came that the Doas wanted someone to move into their village and live with them in order to translate the Bible, the Munnings 'just happened' to be available."

I was humbled by the thought that I might have been the only one in the world praying for the Doa people. That would leave little doubt as to whose prayer God answered.

Now I have a second card taped to the wall. It reminds me to pray for Peter and Mary Jane Munnings—whom I also have never met. But they are helping my friends the Doas, and they need my intercessory prayer support also.

NOTE: If you would like to pray for a Bibleless tribe (there are some 3600 throughout the world), write: Wycliffe Bible Translators, Huntington Beach, California 92648.

When Prayer Comes Alive

Theresa Mulligan

Executive director of Breakthrough; former director, Jews for Jesus; from Lincoln, Virginia

"Pray for Marie in Florida who is seeking healing and restoration for her daughter's marriage . . . there is alcohol and drug involvement . . . three children. . . ." This was my new prayer assignment.

I sat at my kitchen table, Bible and prayer notebook open before me, a pen and a very blank mind. I read and re-read the need. A few names, a shadow of a situation. But how to pray?

Thoughts of my own children came to me, two of them married . . . but I felt no direction for prayer. As an intercessor I had been here before, empty of all imagination, challenged by the complexity of the need before me, seeming so remote and faceless. Where to begin?

Praise and worship. . . . Get into His presence. . . . For the moment forget the need on the breakfast table and praise Him. In His presence I acknowledged my inability to do anything without Him.

"Lord, I ask for wisdom to pray for this hurting family." Then I reminded myself that I was not to pray out of *feelings*, but I was to ask God to give me His compassion for these people whose first names were before me.

In the quiet that followed, phrases of Scripture came to mind: "His name is Faithful and True," "The Good Shepherd."

Then a thought, "Wait for the promise of the Father." The promise of the Father—the Holy Spirit! I opened my hands and offered this precious family to God.

Next came the words: "The Spirit Himself intercedes for us. He helps us in our weakness." My heart began to feel the Father's care for Marie's family, His wisdom for their need. "Father," I asked, "give me a word . . . a promise for Marie." Again, quiet waiting.

A passage from Isaiah came to mind. I opened my Bible to find it: Isaiah 55:6–7 (NIV):

> Seek the Lord while he may be found; call on him
> while he is near. Let the wicked forsake his way and
> the evil man his thoughts. Let him turn to the Lord,
> and he will have mercy on him, and to our God, for
> he will freely pardon.

"O Lord, bring a spirit of repentance to Marie's family and to her daughter's family. Turn them again to Yourself and to Your purposes. Thank You for Your promise of free pardon."

I read on,

> "For my thoughts are not your thoughts, neither are
> your ways my ways," declares the Lord. "As the
> heavens are higher than the earth, so are my ways
> higher than your ways and my thoughts than your
> thoughts."
>
> Verses 8–9

I heard myself pray, "Lord, I felt at a loss in the face of the complexities of Marie's family situation. But Your Word is reminding me that Your ways are greater than mine and that I should expect more than I can think or imagine for Marie." The

51

wings of angels suddenly came under my prayer. The Holy Spirit, the Helper, was with me!

"I stand with Marie for her daughter's marriage, for the breaking from all addictions of her daughter and husband. And, O Lord, for these little ones, for the children . . ."

Perhaps ten minutes later, when the prayer ended, I reflected. The Spirit really does help us in our weakness as we wait on Him.

Praying for that Unborn Child

Ed Corley

Pastor, Berean Gospel Fellowship; from Lincolnton, Georgia

More and more it is accepted that the development of a person's spirit begins in the womb and is designed to be the lifelong fountain from which the soul receives strength and inspiration. It is important, therefore, to pray that the spirit of the unborn baby may be formed properly.

This is especially true because many pregnant mothers have within them a spirit of dejection or rejection or resentment or fear because their own spirits were formed in the wombs of mothers who were dejected or who rejected them or who resented being pregnant. A newborn baby with a normal body may carry in it a wounded and misshapen spirit. So it is very right to pray for the unborn babe, or for the newborn one, to have a rightly formed spirit.

It is also right to pray, even before birth, that the spirit of wisdom be set flowing in the babe's body. The spirit of wisdom can begin its development early (like a stream of pure water flowing underground) and prevent that infant from many a hurtful trial later in life. We all know that a well of water brought to the surface of the ground comes only from a stream that has flowed long underground. If there is no underground water, then there is none to be brought up. So pray that the stream of wisdom may flow "underground" in that babe's spirit, to one day come to the surface and flow openly as wisdom in all affairs of life.

In Luke 1:39–44 we learn that an unborn baby may respond to the Holy Spirit. Mary, newly with child, went up to visit Elizabeth, who was six months pregnant with John the Baptist. When Elizabeth saw Mary, the babe in her womb leaped for joy in response to the Holy Spirit who was moving in the unborn babe in Mary's womb.

Who is to say how early in life the spirit of wisdom is first needed? Even before a child is old enough to be trained in school, he is old enough to have the wisdom not to get in a car with a stranger, not to put something filthy into his mouth, not to walk in a path of danger, not to disobey his parents.

How many sorrows could have been avoided in most lives if only wisdom had begun its work earlier! Prayer for the spirit of that unborn baby could make the crucial difference.

Another Way to Pray

John Sherrill

Author of *My Friend, the Bible;*
co-author of many books including *The Cross and the
Switchblade;* from Westchester
County, New York

Often, walking down the street or driving around town, I
will see a stranger who reminds me of someone I know. Perhaps the individual actually looks like the person I am reminded of, but the trigger can be as subtle as a posture or a
gesture or a hairstyle.

In any event, for years I have put these fleeting resemblances
to special use. I let my memory go to work, bringing up specifics about the person: his smile, his voice, the last conversation we had together. Then I pray. First, briefly, for the stranger
("Bless him today"). Next, for the friend who has been brought
to mind. I have no way of knowing my friend's particular need
at that moment, of course, so I usually pray "in the Spirit,"
trusting that since I do not know how to pray, the Holy Spirit
intercedes for me.

Not too long ago in this way I was reminded of Leonora
Wood, Catherine Marshall LeSourd's mother. My wife, Tib,
and I knew Mrs. Wood for a quarter century and always, when
we visited Evergreen Farm, she was the first person we sought
out. Two specifics would spring to mind as I looked forward to

seeing her: her laugh and the strength of her handshake. Gradually, as she became weakened by age and illness, our visits with Mrs. Wood grew less lengthy. But her laugh and her handclasp were unchanged.

One day I had an occasion to shake hands with another elderly lady in Austria where Tib and I were living for a few months. Her grip was strong and warm, and for an instant I was back in a farmhouse in Virginia. "Thank You, Lord, for our long friendship with Leonora Wood. I ask Your special blessing on her right at this moment." Then, as usual, I prayed for her in the Spirit.

Is there a mystic element in these nudges to intercession, or are these superficial resemblances merely chance reminders, no more?

There is no way of knowing, of course, but the next day I got the hint of an answer. Len LeSourd called us in Austria from Evergreen Farm. He told us that Mrs. Wood was seriously ill and asked for our prayers.

"Len," I was able to say, "your request has already been answered."

NOTE: Mother Wood, at age 97, went to be with the Lord on February 19, 1989.

III
Learning to Listen

When you take seriously the challenge of praying for other people, almost immediately you will make a discovery: You need guidance from God. You need wisdom from Him on how to pray for others. You need to distinguish His voice from other voices that may clamor for your attention.

God has a special heart for us intercessors. He wants very much to have our ear. He will give us specific help as to how we should pray, as He did for the people whose stories follow.

How I Learned to Hear God's Voice

Mark Virkler

Author of *Dialogue with God* and more than fifty other books; from Elma, New York

In recent years I've made an important discovery about prayer. With a little education, a little training and a little stepping back from the sophistication of adulthood any one of us can learn not only to hear and know God's voice, but actually to carry on a two-way dialogue in intimate communion with Him.

You may be saying, "But how can I recognize God's voice?" Probably no question plagues Christians more. For years I searched for the answer. I studied everything I could find in the Bible that indicated how New Testament believers received guidance. I read every book I could find on the voice of God and the gifts of the Holy Spirit. I reasoned that in order to be used by the Spirit in the gifts, particularly the vocal ones, I had to be able to recognize God's voice.

So I listened, as I have said, for the still, small voice, but all I heard were regular thoughts running through my mind. In desperation, I cried, "Where are You, God?" Finally, during a year of searching and studying, the Spirit brought revelation truth to my heart. He showed me that God's voice is sensed as a spontaneous idea appearing in my mind. The key word is *spontaneous*.

The voice of God, I've discovered, is Spirit-to-spirit communication; the Holy Spirit speaking directly to my spirit. It is sensed as a spontaneous thought, idea, word, feeling or vision. Thoughts from my mind, on the other hand, are analytical and cognitive. I reason them out. Thoughts from my heart are spontaneous. It is an intuitive process.

I am *not* saying that every spontaneous thought is the Holy Spirit speaking to us. I *am* saying that spontaneity is heart-level communication, and that analysis and reasoning are mind-level communication. If I want to tune from my head to my heart, therefore, I tune from cognitive, analytical thoughts to the flow of spontaneous thoughts.

When I finally get to my heart, however, I find there are still three "voices" I can hear that need to be distinguished. I can hear those of my own heart, the Holy Spirit's or Satan's. I still have to do some judging and discerning, but at least I have moved from my head to my heart. That in itself is a major accomplishment for many of us in the western world.

Do you remember a time, perhaps when you were driving, when suddenly someone's name popped into your mind and you just knew you were supposed to pray for him? You hadn't been thinking about that person at the time. The thought "just came out of nowhere." But you accepted it as God's prompting you to pray, and you did. That was intercession. When a "chance" thought intersects your reasoning processes, that "chance" encounter is really a divine encounter. God is speaking quietly and easily into your heart.

It was such an exciting revelation to me to realize that I had already heard God speaking to me! Though I had never heard an inner audible voice, I had been aware of ideas lighting upon my mind. They had come simply as spontaneous thoughts. This taught me finally what to listen for to hear God's voice. *When I am listening for the Lord's voice, I am listening for spontaneous thoughts.* I have also found that if I write out these intuitive thoughts, I am amazed at their wisdom.

This is not to say, of course, that this is the only way God can speak. He speaks through His Word. And through circumstances. Occasionally He speaks in an inner audible voice. Once

He called my name and woke me from a sound sleep. I went obediently to my study and began journaling, writing down the spontaneous thoughts as they came to me. On that morning, I sensed God speaking to me in two separate and distinct ways: in an audible voice and through a flow of spontaneous thoughts.

It has taken a definite and deliberate refocusing for me to turn from living in analysis and logic to living in spontaneity. Now as I am driving I worship, I share love with Jesus. I sing Him a love song and allow Him to speak back to me in spontaneous thoughts. I have worked on changing my life so that I am normally tuned in to love and the great Lover of my soul.

I have found that if I remain tuned to spontaneity when I need to think things through or reason them out, the Lord can better interject wisdom and insight. At first I thought that if I "wasted" time loving, I wouldn't be prepared with the answers I needed when I arrived at work. He has taught me, on the contrary, that while I am loving Him, He is rewarding me with productivity, creativity, authority, favor among men, faith and wisdom.

One time the Lord began to speak to me about the need to die to self, to take up my cross. Immediately I thought, *Oh, I know a lot about that! I've preached some good sermons on that very subject!* And I began to write out everything I knew and believed about dying to self. Then I realized what I was doing. My mind had taken over and I was tuned to reason rather than spontaneity. As soon as I became aware of it, I stopped my own thoughts and moved back to intuition. I said, "O.K., Lord, why don't You pick up where You left off? Why don't You tell me what You wanted to say about dying to self?" He did! What He had to say was a little different from what I have believed and taught and it brought adjustment to my life and ministry.

Your spiritual senses will be trained as you use them, and as time goes on you will hear God speaking more easily and frequently. Have you, for instance, ever struggled with a difficult problem when all of a sudden the most creative solution you could imagine popped into your mind? If you have, you probably took credit for coming up with the idea and patted yourself on the back, saying, "Not so dumb after all!" What I've come to see is that such spontaneous, creative solutions to difficult problems that just drop into my mind are not mine at all. They are God's. He is speaking them within me. Rather than take credit for them myself, I now give the glory to God.

I have found that almost everyone has had another type of experience also. Have you ever been in the middle of prayer and had some garbage thoughts defile it? Most people have also taken credit for these thoughts, believing they are their own and feeling guilty and embarrassed. I want to suggest to you that they are probably not your thoughts at all; it is Satan seeking to break up your prayer time. Again, you shouldn't take credit for them or feel guilty or ashamed. I simply tell Satan that I am in the middle of prayer and in Jesus' name to take his garbage thoughts and leave. As I turn my thoughts back to Jesus I sense an immediate release flowing through my heart and mind.

You may be wondering if I am going to recommend throwing our minds away since spontaneous heart-thought is that part of us through which the voice of God so often flows. Not at all! God has given us both our hearts *and* our minds. We are not to despise or overuse either. They are both gifts from almighty God, and they both have a place.

In our culture we have essentially idolized the mind and scorned the heart. Many of us need to repent of that idolization and scorning, and to ask God to balance them out in our lives. That is precisely what I have had to do. Repentance provides the foundation for change, and God has the ability and desire to balance each of us.

What Is God Saying to You?

Leonard LeSourd

Chairman of Breakthrough; former editor, *Guideposts* magazine; associate publisher, Chosen Books; from Lincoln, Virginia

I find myself intrigued and somewhat in awe of the way certain people can not only hear God's voice but will quickly obey His instructions, even in awkward and uncomfortable situations.

Author and teacher Joy Dawson, for example, never gives a teaching, writes a book or accepts a speaking date unless she gets a clear direction from the Lord. Once as a conference speaker she entered an auditorium filled with more than a thousand people and took her place on the platform, praying silently.

Lord, please give me the message you have for this audience.

Silence.

Joy was introduced and stood before the audience with a smile. She explained to them that God's plan was always perfect and that He was obviously trying to teach her and them some new things. She urged the people to pray, along with her, for His word.

I'm sure that many in the audience were surprised, some perhaps annoyed. They prayed. Joy prayed. Time passed— twenty minutes. Forty. Finally, after one hour and ten minutes the Lord directed Joy's thoughts to Lamentations 3:25–26: "The Lord is good to those who wait for Him . . ." (NAS).

The subject of Joy's talk that followed? "Waiting on God."

Some will say, "I'm no Joy Dawson. . . . I could never do that. . . . How would I know when a message was the Lord's?"

There was a time when Joy was that uncertain, too, but she persisted in wanting such a close relationship with the Lord that she would know His voice above all others.

Our tendency is to resist this kind of relationship with Him. It's so threatening. Besides we are often so set in our ways that we do not want change, especially a change that confronts us suddenly. It takes a certain kind of grace, flexibility and self-confidence to alter, in an instant, a plan we've worked on for hours, perhaps days.

That's why I was so impressed by an experience Father Rick Thomas went through several years ago—a classic example of how God's way is always so much better than man's.

Father Rick is one of those gifted Spirit-filled men whose ministry is international—to people of all faiths and no faith. He has spoken eloquently to gatherings of Christian leaders, as well as to civic groups involved with poverty and minority rights in his home town of El Paso, Texas.

At a gathering of several hundred people at a Roman Catholic conference on poverty in a California city, Father Rick got up to make his presentation, a carefully prepared, well-documented speech. As he greeted his audience, the Lord gave him a Scripture: *Acts 2:44–45.* He knew it only too well: *All the believers were together and had everything in common. Selling their possessions and goods, they gave to anyone as he had need* (NIV).

It was a difficult moment for Father Rick because what the Scripture said did not conform with what he was planning to present. After pausing for a moment of prayer, he decided to obey what he felt came from the Lord.

Father Rick quoted the Scripture to his audience, then asked the people: "Are you willing to live out this Scripture?"

The response was a somewhat hesitant yes. Next he asked them all to come to the front of the room and empty the money contained in their wallets and purses for the poor.

Somewhat to his surprise almost everyone in the room did so. The total amount given was more than $10,000.

Next he invited anybody in the room with special needs to come forward and take out of the basket the amount of money they needed. Several people did this.

"The balance left is more than five thousand dollars," he told them. "Now comes the fun part."

The people were divided into small groups, and the money divided among them. Each group was then assigned to go to a certain block in the lowest income section of town. The challenge and adventure: to find families with the greatest needs and give the money, person to person, *with love* and in such a way as not to embarrass them.

The end result was a never-to-be-forgotten experience of giving, a beautiful time together of fellowship and sharing.

How do these stories apply to those of us who have no such discernment or are still learning the ABCs of hearing God's voice? Rather than feel intimidated by the spiritual gifts of a Joy Dawson or a Father Rick Thomas, we need to be challenged to pursue our own walk with the Lord to the point at which we have their fearlessness. My own walk started with small acts of boldness, believing that God did concern Himself with just one person, no matter how insignificant. Gradually I learned to step out in faith in certain situations, to listen as well as pray, to pore over the Scriptures so that I would be familiar with the words He might say to me.

God usually responds to our desire for communication with Him by giving us nudges to do, or not to do, certain things. When we obey there is a blessing. Sometimes it's a time-saver, or a better way to handle a situation. As we grow and learn, the guidance from Him can be momentous. (On one occasion He led me to the woman I was to marry, on another had me resign on faith a position I had held for many years so that I could get into a new field where He wanted me.)

To sum it up, let's ask ourselves the question: "What is God saying to me?" Do I want to hear what He has for me to do? Do I really believe that God's plan for me is so much more exciting and fulfilling than any plan I could possibly concoct for myself?

* * *

While editing a book recently entitled *Learning to Hear God's Voice* by Herman Riffel, I learned the following five guidelines:

1. *Believe that God does speak to us today*

    We are told this in the Bible. Jesus said, "My sheep hear my voice, and I know them, and they follow me" (John 10:27, KJV). Accept this promise at face value and move ahead on faith. (God can speak to us in a number of ways —through a dream, a vision, Scripture, other people, angels—but here I am speaking strictly about hearing His voice.)

2. *Find time to be alone with the Lord*

    Not easy in today's noisy, demanding world. Circumstances will seem to work against you. For most people, the best time is early in the morning before children or others in the household are up. Use this time to pray—and to listen. Do not expect something dramatic or audible. For most, the Lord responds with a thought planted in the mind.

3. *Test what we hear*

    Over a period of time we can learn to distinguish between God's voice and others'. But we must be careful. Satan is a great deceiver. And pride can trip us up. Here are three tests:

    a. Check the guidance received against the Scriptures. God will not tell us anything that goes against His Word.

    b. Seek confirmation from at least two other Christians before taking any action. Paul tells us in Thessalonians "to examine everything carefully."

    c. Be open to checks and corrections from your church and pastor. Granted, this may not work if there is division and controversy in your church, but if you belong to a body of believers that functions effectively, it can be very helpful.

4. *Keep a journal of what God says*

    It is because men and women kept a record of their experiences with God that we have a Bible. David kept a record of the songs he wrote: These psalms have inspired people down through the ages.

No one sought more diligently to receive God's instructions than my late wife, Catherine Marshall LeSourd. She filled the pages of dozens of journals over a fifty-year period, a priceless source of knowledge and wisdom.

The journal should be a record of our spiritual journey— prayers offered up and answers and insights from God. As we go back through our journals, we can evaluate the guidance received, and better see what was really from God and what was not.

5. *Obey God*

There is no point in seeking God's guidance for our lives—or for others we are praying for—if we do not act upon His instructions. Obedience was hard for Moses as he led the Israelites toward the Promised Land, but when he did not obey God, there was trouble and when he did obey, there were blessings.

It works the same for us today. If a word from the Lord seems unusual or difficult, we should go through the tests. If still in doubt, we should ask God to confirm what He wants us to do.

To sum it up, to hear what God is trying to say to us, we must *believe* He will speak to us, *make time alone* with Him, *test* what we hear, *record* it in our journals and then *obey* Him. The payoff is a relationship with Him that surpasses anything else in life.

IV
Overcoming Obstacles in Your Prayer Life

As you move into regular intercession, you will begin to discover areas in your life that are blocking the flow of power. Don't be thrown by this. We all have our areas of weakness. Satan will try to discourage you at this point, defeat you if he can. Always remember this: As an intercessor you are in a position of power and authority.

Call upon Jesus Christ, the divine Intercessor, for help. Claim the authority He gives you *to stand against the enemy*, renouncing the spirits of pride or criticalness or unforgiveness or manipulation or whatever is blocking you—as the following people have done.

A Fast on Criticalness

Catherine Marshall

Founder of Breakthrough, author of fifteen books including *A Man Called Peter* and *Christy*

I have long since learned that my day gets off to a poor start unless I can begin it by being alone with the Lord for at least a few minutes of worship and prayer. During this time often I ask, "Lord, do You have any special word for me today?"

One morning His answer was especially clear and to say the least, startling. He reminded me of a Scripture passage I had not thought of in a long time: "So let us stop criticizing one another . . ." (Romans 14:13, MOFFATT). My assignment: For one day I was to go on a "fast" from criticism. I was not to criticize anybody about anything.

A confession is in order here. I am inclined to be a perfectionist and have, therefore, always been a highly critical person.

Into my mind crowded all the usual objections: "But then what happens to value-judgments? You Yourself, Lord, spoke of 'righteous judgment.' What does that mean? How could society operate without critiques?"

All such resistance was brushed aside. *Just obey Me without questioning: an absolute fast on any critical statements for this day.*

As I pondered this assignment I realized there was an even humorous side to this kind of fast. What did the Lord want to show me?

For the first half of the day, I simply felt a void, almost as if I had been wiped out as a person. This was especially true at luncheon with Len, my mother and my secretary, Jeanne Sevigny, present. Several topics came up about which I had definite opinions. I listened to the others and kept silent. Barbed comments on the tip of my tongue about certain world leaders were suppressed. In our talkative family no one seemed to notice.

Bemused, I noticed that my comments were not missed. The federal government, the judicial system and the institutional church could get along nicely without my penetrating observations. But still I didn't see what this fast on criticism was accomplishing—until mid-afternoon.

For several years I had been praying for one talented young man whose life had gotten sidetracked. Perhaps my prayers for him had been too negative. That afternoon, a specific, positive vision for this life was dropped into my mind with God's unmistakable hallmark on it—joy.

Ideas began to flow in a way I had not experienced in years. Now it was apparent what the Lord wanted me to see. My critical nature had been stifling creativity—perhaps even the ideas that He wanted to give me.

The following Sunday night in a Bible study, sharing group, I told of my day's-fast experiment. The response was startling. Many admitted that criticalness was one of the chief problems in their offices or in their marriages or with their teenage children.

My own character flaw here is not going to be corrected overnight. But in thinking this through, I find the most solid scriptural basis possible for it. The Greek word translated "criticize" in Moffatt is rendered "judge" or "judging" in the King James Version. All through the Sermon on the Mount, Jesus sets Himself squarely against our seeing other people and life situations through this negative lens.

More experimenting is needed with this type of fast. Perhaps we intercessors could share our further discoveries with one another as we do so. What I've learned so far can be summed up as follows:

1. A critical spirit focuses us in on ourselves and makes us unhappy. We lose perspective and humor.
2. A critical spirit blocks the positive creative thoughts God longs to give us.
3. A critical spirit can prevent good relationships between individuals and often produces retaliatory criticalness.
4. Criticalness blocks the positive attributes of the Spirit of God—love, good will, mercy.
5. Whenever we see something wrong in another person, rather than criticize him or her directly, or talk to others about this person, we might ask the Spirit of God to do the correction work needed.

This Scripture seems to wrap it up for me:

> So we do not criticize at all; the hour of reckoning has still to come, when the Lord will come to bring dark secrets to the light and to reveal life's inner aims and motives. Then each of us will get his meed of praise from God.
>
> 1 Corinthians 4:5, MOFFATT

In Place of Criticism

Oswald Chambers warns us, "We see where other folks are failing, and we turn our discernment into the gibe of criticism instead of into intercession on their behalf. He reveals things in order that we may take the burden of these souls before Him and form the mind of Christ about them."

When Christ touches us and brings us alive in the spirit, He gives us a more sensitive discernment about others—something we cannot have unless we first "stop criticizing one another."

The Cost of Unforgiveness

Charles C. Carrin

Pastor, Grace Fellowship; from
Delray Beach, Florida

In my ministry I am finding more and more that people who hold unforgiveness toward others are reducing their prayer power and forfeiting their own help from the Lord. That statement may seem harsh, but Jesus taught it very plainly. He said, "If ye forgive not men their trespasses, neither will your heavenly Father forgive your trespasses." Later He intensified this warning when He told of the person who was "delivered unto the tormentors" because he refused to forgive another.

Simply stated, it comes to this: If we want deliverance from our ills, we must clear our own records and totally forgive all others who have harmed us. Jesus also taught that we should not attempt to worship God until all our unforgiveness has been dealt with. "If you come to the altar to offer your sacrifice," He said, "and then remember that your brother has a grievance with you, leave your sacrifice unoffered. Go, first be reconciled to your brother, and then make your offering to God" (see Matthew 5:23–24).

A deeply troubled woman came to us for private ministry and counseling. She was abusing her children to the point where she was frightened by her own conduct. Yet she seemed powerless to stop. I was led to ask her, "Who is it that you have not forgiven?"

When the woman said she was clear in this area, we attempted to minister the authority of Jesus' name on her behalf. But nothing happened.

The woman became frantic for help; she cried, she prayed. She was tormented by fear, yet our ministry failed to bring deliverance.

Frequently in such cases the Holy Spirit speaks a "word of knowledge" to us and reveals an old injury that has been walled off but never forgiven. In this case it was caused by an uncle. When this root of unforgiveness was exposed, we heard her sob out, "But I can't forgive him! He hurt me so badly—I don't feel I can ever forgive him!"

We lovingly explained that forgiving one another is not a feeling, it is an act of the will. One may not feel like going to work but one *can* and *does*. If unforgiveness is the only cause of delay in the woman's deliverance, and she tells the Lord, "I *do* forgive him," Satan's legal hold on her will be broken and the woman will experience immediate freedom. Her problem of child abuse ended at the very moment she forgave her uncle.

In cases where psychiatry has failed after months of treatment, we have seen people come to instant deliverance through forgiveness. Jesus' methods work.

The woman's situation is understood in this way: Because she did not forgive, she retained the hatred of her uncle's sin in her own life. That hatred bound her to Satan and exposed her to his continued harassment. The moment she turned loose of the hatred by forgiving the uncle, she was free. Her ability to pray returned.

No matter how painful the injury, we *must* forgive. In fact, the deeper the injury, the more vital it is that we forgive. We have no other choice.

A wife must forgive the husband who abandoned her and the children for another woman. Whether or not she ever sees him again is not the question. She *must* forgive him—or destroy herself.

A man must forgive the business partner who cheated and destroyed his financial holdings.

Parents must forgive the drunk driver who killed their child.

A husband must forgive the doctor whose blunder cost the life of his wife.

It is imperative that we learn this: Our forgiving others is not a luxury we extend to them. It is what God requires of us for our own good, our own protection, our own blessing. God knows the deadliness of unforgiveness. He knows that unforgiveness is Satan's open door to invade and destroy our lives. Satan can do this because he always causes unforgiveness to resurface again in the form of anxiety, irritability, arthritis, hypertension, migraine, ulcers, cancer, organ malfunction, early death and a host of other devilish ills.

Check your record all the way back to childhood. Clean out the closet. First be reconciled to others, forgive everyone and then ask God for the help you need. Get down on your knees and do it now. Otherwise, the price you pay for unforgiveness is your own personal torment. This price is high, much too high!

Working Through the Dry Period

Betsy Weight

Prayer warrior and freelance writer; from Eskdale, Utah

Why do you resist writing about "the spiritually dry period?"

The question came to me one morning as I realized my inner unrest was the Holy Spirit drawing my attention to Him and admonishing me to, "stand still and listen" (see 1 Samuel 9:27).

I turned off the vacuum cleaner and rehearsed a list of excuses before the Lord, all logical reasons why I had ignored a suggestion to write about "The Dry Period."

After hearing me through, He spoke softly again and asked, *Now, what is your real reason?*

I fell on my face before Him and confessed my fears. As God has opened the way for me to grow and mature in Him, His presence has become "like the dew of [lofty] Mount Hermon, and the dew that comes on the hills of Zion" (Psalm 133:3, TAB). This dew is a delicate, crystalline beauty in my life that appears so fragile in this pressurized capsule of life called "time." I know His promise is that He will never leave me or forsake me, but when the lovely freshness of the "dew" is gone, God can seem so distant, life so dry. Furthermore, the absence of His Spirit leaves an emptiness I cannot define.

In recent months, I have found that every shared testimony of His work in me has been subjected to severe testing in my own life. I told Him I feared writing and then was tested through "dryness," as when he departed King Hezekiah, "to try him, that he might know all that was in his heart" (2 Chronicles 32:31, KJV). I did not want to be left without the strength and joy of "knowing" His presence. I asked forgiveness for my fear and expressed my earnest desire to be open and receptive to His Word.

As I waited in silence before Him, I heard the words, *I THIRST!* Then I saw that as the sin of mankind was laid upon Jesus, as He gave Himself up to die on the cross in our place, the Holy Father would no longer even look upon Him. Jesus, who knew no sin (1 Peter 2:22), who was Himself the Source of "living water" (John 7:38), was separated from the glory of His Father and left alone. Forsaken! As He hung on the cross, He experienced the deepest and most awesome thirst ever known to man. In that moment of extreme suffering, He cried out, "I thirst" (John 19:28), and then in total relinquishment said, "Father, into Your hands I commit my spirit" (Luke 23:46, TAB).

As the impact of this scene sank deep into my spirit, I was given further Scripture: "He that saith he abideth in him ought himself also so to walk, even as he walked" (1 John 2:6, KJV). Jesus asked the disciples who desired to sit at His right hand in glory if they were "able to drink the cup that I drink, or be baptized with the baptism [of affliction] with which I am baptized" (Mark 10:38, TAB). On the cross, Jesus declared His thirst, and then submitted all to the Father. To the eyes of the world, He was dead, "He saved others; himself he cannot save" (Matthew 27:42, KJV). But it was in that final submission to the will of God that He was lifted up where we now see Him seated at the right hand of the Father (see Hebrews 1:3) . . . seated in the holiest place where the "water" never ceases to flow from beneath the throne . . . that abiding place in God *where there is no dryness.*

I have thought again about the dew and God's Word, "I will be as the dew and the night mist to Israel; he shall grow and blossom as the lily, and cast forth his roots as [the sturdy evergreens of] Lebanon" (Hosea 14:5, TAB). God grants the freshness of the dew, His manifest presence in our lives, to strengthen and encourage us; but we are to cast our roots down to the very source of life where we can draw freely from Him without fear of surface conditions (see Jeremiah 17:8). Can our way of sacrifice be any less than that of Jesus if we are to be seated with Him in glory?

Times of dryness will come. The supreme test, and His obedience to the will of the Father in that test, brought Jesus to His place of supreme glory and honor—seated in majesty at the right hand of God. The pattern is there. Our times of testing will lead to times of refreshing as we submit, send our roots deeper and trust God through every circumstance.

Prepare ahead for the dry times. Know the Word of God and plant His will in your heart. "Be strong in the Lord—be empowered through your union with Him; draw your strength from Him—that strength which His [boundless] might provides" (Ephesians 6:10, TAB).

The Problem with Pride

David Wilkerson

Pastor, Times Square Church;
author of a number of books including *The Cross and the Switchblade*; from New York City

Do you recognize pride in yourself?

Many Christians would admit, "Well, I may be self-
assured—even confident. At the worst I may see myself as
more talented or intelligent than others. But I'm not proud! I
give God all the credit for what I've accomplished and for
who I am. It's all in His strength. I open my heart to be
searched by His Word. If I was prideful, surely He would
have shown it to me."

Recently the Holy Spirit spoke to my heart about this sin. I
said, "Lord, You mean You want me to preach a message about
pride at the Times Square Church, don't You? There must be
pride in the congregation."

The Spirit's answer stunned me. *No, David, I want to speak to
you about pride, about the subtle kinds of pride that you yourself are
guilty of. First you must see it in your own heart, then you may preach
it to others.*

Like most other Christians, I thought I was at least trying to
be humble. We take care not to boast like Pharisees about being
better than all the rest. But deep within our hearts we think,

"I'm not arrogant, boastful or overly ambitious. So how could I be proud?"

Lately, the Word has been dealing with me, exposing forms of pride I did not know could be so deeply embedded in me, revealing to me how pride blocks the power of prayer.

When the Spirit said, *Pride in you, David,* I replied, "But, Lord, I'm not trying to be somebody great! You know that. I'm not a braggart or a boaster. I am honestly trying to decrease so Christ can increase. If there is pride in me, I can't even see it. Please show it to me. Expose it to me!"

So He showed me! As I look back I tremble at how many times I committed this hateful sin. I am guilty of it.

God sees pride in an entirely different way than we do. He showed me that I had too narrow a definition of pride. Yes, there is a wicked, boastful, arrogant pride, and it can be seen all about us in these days. But there is also a pride that is spiritual in nature. It is committed by those who have walked closely with God and it can be seen in the holiest among us. The more spiritual you are, the more revelation you have had, the closer to Him that you have been, the more hideous this sin is when it is committed. It is not a way of life, although it could become so. It is a sin that is often committed even on our knees, wholly seeking God.

Pride is independence—humility is dependence.

Pride rushes in to take matters into its own hands. One of the greatest temptations true Christians face is getting ahead of God. It is acting without a clear mandate from God.

Pride is impatience.

Pride is repelled by the idea of servanthood. Today everybody wants to be everything but a servant. The big children's game in America used to be "Masters of the Universe"! But that is also becoming the theology of many Christians.

The great ones also serve. Paul said he was "a servant of Jesus Christ" (Romans 1:1, KJV). James called himself "a servant . . . of the Lord Jesus" (James 1:1). And Christ, the Lord, the very Son of God, "made himself of no reputation, and took upon him the form of a servant, and was made in the likeness of men. . . . He humbled himself, and became obedient unto death, even the death of the cross" (Philippians 2:7–8, KJV).

Examine yourself as I have. Lay your prideful ways at the foot of the cross. Jesus will help you see how to turn pride into servanthood.

The sure cure for the sin of pride is to become a servant to those around you.

When Prayer Is Manipulation

Germaine Copeland

Author of *Prayers that Avail Much* and *God Answers Prayer*; from Atlanta, Georgia

In your prayer for someone close to you, have you ever gotten in the way of what God wanted to do? It has probably happened to all of us. It certainly has to me. One way it can take place is through a misunderstanding of the following Scripture:

> Again I say unto you, That if two of you shall agree on earth as touching any thing that they shall ask, it shall be done for them of my Father which is in heaven.   Matthew 18:19, KJV

The Lord taught me much about this Scripture after a vivid experience in my marriage. At that time my husband, Everette, did not seem to be interested in the work God had called me to do. (I was seeking more and more of Jesus, and would go with friends or alone to meetings to hear various Bible teachers.) Although he refused to go with me to these meetings, Everette did not hinder me from going.

After a while the desire for my husband to attend these meetings with me became a consuming fire within me. Many times when alone, I cried all the way to a service because I wanted my life's partner by my side.

Everette continued to ignore all my pleas until finally I took this situation to my intercessory prayer group. After I had presented my heartfelt desire for Everette, the intercessors entered into that prayer of agreement with me for my husband to attend a particular seminar. There was no doubt in my mind now that Everette would go. I believed the Bible: Hadn't Jesus said that "anything" that we ask in agreement would be done for us of the Father?

The first two nights of the meeting came and went. Everette stayed at home and I attended with friends. Finally, it was the third and closing night of the meeting—God's last chance to answer our "binding" prayer of agreement. Two seats were reserved in the front row of the auditorium—one for me, and one for my husband. As the time for the service approached that evening, I turned down all offers of a ride to the meeting because I just *knew* that my night of triumph had arrived.

It was past time to leave for the meeting and I was still waiting, sure that Everette was going. Finally, he turned to me and said, "If you are going to the service tonight, you'd better leave. You're already late."

I struggled to open my mouth in protest that he just *had* to go with me, but before I could form the words, he closed the subject: "You need to know that you and your friends cannot 'confess' me into going. My mind is made up; I am staying home to watch the World Series on television."

At the meeting I was met by an usher who walked me down that long aisle to the reserved seats while everyone's eyes followed me step by step. I knew that God could not fail, so I was convinced that we must have missed God somewhere.

There had been no lack of zeal on *my* part—or that of the intercessors. But there was also no Everette at the meeting. Where had we gone amiss?

The problem was that our zeal for God was not enlightened according to vital knowledge—revelation knowledge. We had misused the prayer of agreement. We had taken Scripture out of context, "confessed" our own selfish desire and then expected God to act in response to our misguided faith. He won't do it. God will not move contrary to His Word in order to answer an improper prayer.

The Holy Spirit began to do His work of enlightenment in me. One word kept coming to my mind. He was showing me that what my prayer partners and I had engaged in was not spiritual intercession but *manipulation*. Our "spiritual prayer of agreement" had actually been nothing more than an act of the flesh—one of which Paul refers to in Galatians 5:20 as "witch-craft"! We had tried to control another person's actions by use of the intellect through prayer and positive confession. I realized that it was not my friends' agreement that I had needed in that situation—it was Everette's!

That night when I released my husband's "freedom of choice" to God, I, too, was set free. I realized that my husband was not against me, but for me. I returned to him what he had given me—the freedom to hear from God and to obey the voice of the Good Shepherd *as an individual*.

The very next year another seminar was scheduled, and to my surprise Everette not only attended voluntarily, he also served as an usher by his own volition. I went with him to all the evening services.

When You Feel Far from God

Sondra Johnson

Communications director, Breakthrough; administrator of Christian Guidance and Counseling
Center; from Hillsboro, Virginia

For the past two years, my family has experienced more than its share of turmoil, including serious problems with two teenagers, topped off by my husband's losing a job he had held for nearly 23 years. We had been without income for eight months when Larry announced that we were going to make our annual trek to the ocean. I was resistant. Living on a small working farm, we did not have the kind of lifestyle that permits us to up and leave at a moment's notice, even in the best of times.

Still, I had seen the look on the faces of our two youngest children when their daddy mentioned their beloved beach. Also, I knew that much as we had tried to shield them from worry, they were well aware of quite a large portion of our problems and heartaches.

If Larry thought we could manage a vacation, who was I to say no?

So when we arrived at the beach, I was tense and out of sorts. Through all the problems that had beset us, I was having nagging doubts about my worthiness as a Christian. From somewhere deep within, I had begun to question whether or not I was failing God and therefore was the cause of our two years of frustration.

One evening as the four of us drove back from dinner along the coastal highway, no one could agree on where we should spend the evening. It seemed to my aching head that the argument had gone on all day. I felt trapped between my husband's desires and those of our children. I understood their feelings, for I had been a child at this very beach, yet I knew Larry needed my support. Something broke inside me and I heard myself announce tearfully, "This is going to be my last year at this beach." Everyone rode the rest of the way to the hotel in silence.

The next morning I awoke before dawn. It was barely 4:30 A.M. My head still ached. As I dozed, bits of my life appeared before me like the coming attractions flash on the screen at the movies. These were not happy events in my life, but everything I had ever done wrong or felt guilty about. As I watched these scenes, I dipped into a state of depression.

Finally, to be free of the pain in my head and the replay of painful moments in my life, I rose, dressed and stepped outside.

The sea air was chilly and damp. The sand was cold as I began my walk down the beach. No one was in sight as far as I could see in any direction. *How constant the sea is,* I thought. I'd been coming here nearly every summer since I was three years old. Nothing had changed . . . even the sandbar I remembered as a child. Ahead of me, the sun began burning its way through thick gray and white clouds, with streams of light seeping around the edges.

Suddenly, I smiled. As I let the cold ocean lap over my feet and ankles, I felt pure joy when the sand washed back over my toes. Then, there in front of me, was the largest shell I had ever seen on this beach. I scooped it up and put it into the bag I had brought with me.

On down the beach I went, picking up shells and talking to the seagulls that raced the waves in search of food. As the sun broke from behind the clouds, I burst into song. "Amazing

Grace," I sang to the noisy waves, "how sweet the sound, that saved a wretch like me!"

It occurred to me that everyone at one time or another felt as I had been feeling—like a wretch. "It is no secret what God can do—what He's done for others, He'll do for you; with arms wide open, He'll pardon you. . . ." As I sang I knew I needed once again to relinquish all to God and *let* Him do for me.

Most of the shells along the beach were broken, just like most of the people I know. But, like these people, the shells' reason for being was not over just because they were broken. Because of the continual pounding of the surf, these broken shells will one day be sand, soft and smooth, just like the sand that was now warm beneath my feet, each grain necessary to the whole. Many of the people (including me) will also become smooth, reshaped, battered not by waves, but by circumstances of life . . . yet able to continue as new creatures in God, each one important to the body of Christ.

As I turned to retrace my steps to the hotel, a dark shell caught my eye. I almost passed over it because I saw that it was not whole, but something made me stoop and reach into the water that threatened to wash it back to sea. As I picked it up, I saw that the piece broken out had left the shape of a perfect heart.

Astonished, I looked at it carefully. I felt as though God had sent me a valentine.

Suddenly my burden lightened. The scenes I had witnessed earlier that morning no longer hurt. Tears stung my eyes—not tears of sadness, but tears of joy that my God was still with me. Feeling completely new, I quickened my step, anxious to get back to my family and share my treasures.

The sun danced on the waves like diamonds. "Good morning," someone called as he jogged by me. He was running to strengthen his heart. God and I were walking together now to strengthen mine.

V
Combat in the Heavenlies

Intercession is spiritual warfare. The moment you aim a prayer to the Lord and divine Intercessor, action begins in the heavenly Kingdom. In some cases protecting angels are dispatched. We do not know the specifics, but it is not hard to imagine what is going on in the unseen world if you are deep into Scripture. Satan's forces are hurt by your prayers. The stronger the prayer power, the weaker the enemy becomes.

The Daily Call to Spiritual Warfare

Leonard LeSourd

Chairman of Breakthrough; former editor, *Guideposts* magazine; associate publisher, Chosen Books; from Lincoln, Virginia

The letter arrived at Breakthrough from Hilda who lives in Texas. She asked us to pray for Ron, her nineteen-year-old son who was living with Jennifer, his girlfriend. Both were involved with drugs. "I've done everything I can think of to rescue my son," Hilda wrote.

The moment our coordinator, Pam, opened and read the letter, the warfare of intercession began. Pam prayed, then was directing the prayer request to five intercessors scattered about the country when a call came from her husband at home. "The plumber fixed the leak in the sink, but says the floorboards underneath have rotted and need to be replaced," he reported.

Another expense, Pam thought to herself. *If I wasn't working, these things wouldn't happen.* The day before she had to leave early to pick up a sick child at school. A wave of negative thoughts suddenly engulfed her.

Stop it! Pam rebuked the thoughts in the name of Jesus, for He was the one who had led her to Breakthrough. All her friends and family had agreed that an intercession ministry here was God's appointment for her.

When Rosemary, one of the five intercessors, received the letter from Breakthrough with Hilda's request, she put it aside. *I'll get to that later*, she thought. For she had just received a disquieting report from her doctor. Her blood sugar content was too high. Fear thoughts took over.

Stop it! Rosemary is an experienced intercessor. She knows when the enemy is attacking her thought life. She reached for the letter about Hilda and went to her bedroom to pray.

"Those little harassments are coincidences," say the skeptics.

"Not so," say those who are veteran prayer warriors. "We've come to expect them. We can almost measure the importance of our prayer efforts by the number of little things that go wrong in our daily lives when we're involved in all-out intercession."

As Rosemary was praying for Hilda's Ron and Jennifer, an insight came to her. She wrote it out and mailed it to the Breakthrough office: "Hilda needs to show more love and less judgment toward this young couple." Then she cited some verses in the thirteenth chapter of 1 Corinthians. We evaluated the material, agreed that it might be helpful and sent it on to Hilda. The anonymity of everyone was protected so that there were no telephone calls for counsel. The focus is on prayer alone.

In our prayer warfare at Breakthrough sometimes we learn the result, sometimes not. Hilda's request resulted in several answers. Two months later Ron broke off the relationship and began dating a Christian girl. Hilda acknowledged that the insight from Rosemary was right on target—she had been too controlling with her son. The change in him came after she pulled back from the situation, using just love and prayer. And the moment Rosemary began concentrating on her intercession assignments, her own health improved.

It is important to understand that we at Breakthrough are not people who see Satan behind every door or who credit all our mistakes and misdeeds to him. I personally believe we are born as fallible creatures, are prone to error and will go through life wreaking havoc upon ourselves and others unless we learn to be disciplined. But I also know from personal experience that there is an enemy, a force of evil, that intrudes into our thoughts (and lives) to tempt, to confuse and to discourage us. His goal—to render us ineffective, to destroy our reputations and even our lives.

How do we fight back?

First, know that the ultimate victory was won when Christ took on the sins of all of us as He was nailed to the cross. To some people under heavy attack, this victory seems almost irrevelant for the here and now. It is not, though. Knowing who the Victor is helps one fight harder. We need to understand that *God is allowing a defeated Satan to vent his rage and frustration on the world for a time period, known only to Him, and for reasons of His own.* But we as God's people can move ahead with the sure knowledge of the ultimate result.

Second, we are given a mighty tool—prayer. When God's people begin to pray, Satan falters, for he knows he cannot win against such weapons. This is why Satan is so actively opposed to those who pray, particularly intercessors.

Check yourself here. How much resistance do you feel in your spirit to going to church, a Bible study or even witnessing as compared to using a major piece of your time for intensive prayer? The enemy will try to distract or disrupt you because *he does not want you to pray for others.*

Daniel the prophet was a great prayer warrior. Once he spent three weeks in prayer and fasting. At the end of this prayer time an angel appeared to him and said, "Do not be afraid, Daniel, for from the first day that you . . . [humbled] yourself before your God, your words were heard, and I have come in response" (Daniel 10:12, NAS).

Why did it take the angel three weeks to get there? The angel explained his delay: "The prince of the kingdom of Persia [Satan] was withstanding me for twenty-one days; then behold, Michael . . . [the Archangel] came to help me" (verse 13). That's spiritual warfare in the heavenly kingdom.

This scriptural reference to Daniel's three weeks of prayer was the basis for our decision at Breakthrough to send out each request for three weeks of prayer. If more prayer is needed, we will ask the same or a different group of intercessors to continue for another three weeks. It is celebration time when we learn that a prayer is answered, as with Hilda.

Intercession is spiritual warfare. Prayer is the weapon. Mind-boggling when you think that our prayers can result in the dispatching of angels to trouble spots, in the repositioning of heavenly forces, in a life being saved. That is why God is so urgently in need of intercessors.

Extra Power in a Crisis

Jean Ware

Prayer warrior; from Corpus Christi, Texas

At 9:15 P.M. my Bible study teacher felt a sudden call to intercession. She went before the Lord with tears and groanings (Romans 8:26).

At 9:35 on that same Sunday evening last year, I had gone into the living room to watch a Christian program on television. My husband, a family physician, was away on medical duties. Suddenly I was aware of something or someone behind me. As I turned, a man in a crouched position was silhouetted for a few seconds against the light. He grabbed me from behind and held a long dagger-type knife to my stomach. His head was covered with a hood with slits cut for the eyes. As his arm went around my throat, he told me not to make a sound and in very vulgar terms made his intentions of rape known. He tied a towel very tightly around my head so that I was unable to see anything.

I was terrified and shocked beyond measure. For the past eighteen months, there had been a series of nine rapes in my neighborhood. There was a great deal of fear circulating. The police were holding neighborhood meetings to advise people about protecting themselves. Extra patrol cars had been assigned to our area, and plainclothes policemen were riding around on bikes in an attempt to stop the attacker. This intruder had slipped by them all.

After he tied my head, he threw me down on the couch. As I prayed, I can't begin to describe the sudden presence of Jesus at this time. It was so gentle and natural—as if I were not even a part of what was going on. I heard myself telling the attacker, "I love you. You are a fine young man. I will do anything I can to help you, but I cannot be a part of this."

The words were not condemning, not panicky, excited or emotional—just gentle, flowing words, like living water being poured out in words of love. But I didn't love this man. My body was terrified in shock, my mind was jelly. It was the Holy Spirit ministering through me to this man, waging all-out spiritual warfare in my behalf.

The man became very angry, kept telling me to shut up.

"Please forgive me," I said, "but I can't stop talking."

He became more angry as I consistently, but gently, resisted his action. The spiritual words continued to pour out.

He put a gun to my face, after hitting me on the head with it, and said, "I'm going to blow your head off."

I believed him. I felt that my death was very close, yet it seemed very normal and easy. I just thought, *You and me, Lord.* I reached up to Jesus to touch the hem of His garment and began praying in the Spirit out loud. When I did, it was as if this man had hit a brick wall. He stopped and said, "I'm leaving. Stay here ten minutes and don't move. . . . How do I get out of this house?" A spirit of confusion had gripped him.

"I'm sorry, I can't think right now." I couldn't even remember how to get out of my own house. He left on his own.

As soon as I could, I got up and ran to a neighbor's home. The police arrived within minutes at 10:30 P.M. They were so courteous and gentle in questioning me; they were thorough in going over the house. They collected evidence from the garden, mud, plants and fingerprints on the furniture. Until 2:00 A.M. they searched. My deepest appreciation goes to the Corpus Christi Police Department for their sensitive treatment of me throughout the investigation.

After they left I went to bed and cried out to the Lord, "Lord, I really don't understand." Jesus reminded me, as in the Scripture, I am body, soul and spirit. While my body and soul experienced everything completely during the attack, my spirit was at peace with Him. My spirit remained untouched.

Blessed Jesus! Holy, holy, holy is Thy name, Lord! I was the tenth to be attacked, but the only one not raped. I was also that man's last victim. Eleven days later the police arrested him at a Little League baseball game and charged him with aggravated sexual assault. He was on probation for the same offense when he was arrested. Now he is back in prison to serve a 65-year sentence. Since all this happened, Jesus has never been so close to me. I have no hard feelings toward that man. A friend of mine said, "How can you say that about such an evil person?" My answer is that I felt the love of Jesus for him. So the story for him is unfinished.

Later I discovered that my Bible study leader had been called to prayer just before the attack, not knowing for whom she prayed. Now, of course, it is so clear to us both. Praise God for her faithfulness in prayer. Jesus is teaching us how to act as one body, instead of separate parts.

The Lord continues to use friends, acquaintances and even complete strangers to minister to me. At a recent Full Gospel Business Men's Convention, I was given these words:

> It was a sacrifice to Me.
> I will heal your wounds.

In *The Vine Life* by Colleen Townsend Evans, I learned that fruit must be sacrificed, the grapes crushed, for new wine to be poured out for others. As Jesus heals my wounds, I share this experience with those who might be hurting or afraid—always looking over their shoulders, fearful of going into the yard to water the garden, leaving the house, going into an elevator, answering the door. For all those carrying a burden of fear, may I affirm and reaffirm this truth: *Jesus can be trusted with your life.*

When We Are Called to Battle

David Hazard

Award-winning writer and professional editor; from Northern Virginia

Several years ago while driving through New York State on a winter day, I was treated to a marvelous "show" in the western sky ahead of me. The sun was sinking through mountains of billowing clouds, its fiery glow turning them to breathtaking shades. Inwardly, it seemed that God was pointing out each color. *The red is for My blood. Purple speaks of My kingly power. And gold—the gold is to remind you of My heavenly treasures, which I will pour out for you.*

The awesomeness of God swept me up and my spirit soared in praise. Somehow I sensed I was being given keys of some sort, especially when the curious words formed within: *Don't forget in the darkness what you have heard in the light.* What could it mean?

As night came on, my thoughts turned to my brother, Dick. There wasn't time to see him on this trip, yet Dick had been on my mind a lot recently. He was going through some tough times, but of more concern to me was his uncertain faith and beliefs. Then when I started to pray for him, a strange thing happened. It was as though the cold and darkness dropped like blankets over my words, muffling them. Where I had felt peace and joy before, I now felt turmoil.

As the mile markers rushed by, in me the darkness and concern increased until I was crying out to God. Was something bad happening to my brother? Even as I cried out, a more immediate problem arose: First, my headlights grew dim; soon the dash lights were fading, too. Now real darkness was closing in on the prayer battle I seemed to be waging for my brother.

That was when it struck me: Perhaps I *was* in a spiritual battle. Perhaps the nagging feelings about Dick were the Holy Spirit's signal that I should be praying harder. But how?

It was then the words returned to me: *Don't forget in the darkness what you have heard in the light.* And I remembered the description of the clouds.

Red for the blood of Christ, making the way clear for us to approach God. Nothing can hinder our prayers from reaching the Father. *Purple,* the sign that His kingly power is activated by our prayers, vanquishing every darkness. And *gold* for victory—the treasure of blessings prayer brings.

At once, I felt that I was bearing a tricolored standard into the thick of a battle. I was not going to rehearse all the facts of my brother's situation—or worry about what "might" be going wrong. I determined to praise and thank God for His sacrifice, power and triumph in all things.

And that's what I did as I pulled behind a tractor trailer and followed it the last few miles to my exit. I continued my "prayer standard" even when my car died half a mile from home and I was given a lift by two men who turned out to be drunk! By then, I was determined that no darkness, no worry, would win over me.

Stepping inside the door well after midnight, I was surprised to see my landlord waiting up in a rumpled bathrobe. Even more surprised when he said, "Call your brother back. It sounded urgent."

But nothing could compare with the feeling when I heard Dick's voice at the other end of the line. "David," he began with some emotion, "tonight I met a friend of yours. He began talking to me about Christ—and I didn't want to hear it at first. I guess I was fighting it. But something happened. Tonight I prayed and gave my life to Jesus Christ." He paused. "David, are you there?"

I could not answer for the lump in my throat. How could I begin to explain what was going through my heart? The joy. And the wonder that somehow I, in a car miles from home, had taken part in winning the spiritual battle that had raged that evening over the soul of my brother.

Can Our Prayers Change God's Mind?

Brother Andrew

Author of *God's Smuggler*;
founder of Open Doors; from
Santa Ana, California

My favorite definition of intercession is: *Doing battle with God when He has already made up His mind.*

This may startle you. Certainly, for someone with a Calvinistic background like mine, it is difficult to think that God's mind can be changed. After all, He knows all that is going to happen, and He has made up His mind about it.

Or has he?

Is everything determined beforehand? Are God's mind and will static?

If you feel that this is the case, and that this is the way God *ought* to be, then you could easily become a Muslim, for the religion of Islam has this highly fatalistic quality to it, as do other eastern religions.

Do you realize that Christianity is the only religion in the world in which you are allowed to disagree with God? You dare not do that in any other religion. We Christians, and especially those who have taken up the ministry of intercession, have a special privilege!

Unfortunately, throughout history, there has been a pious

acceptance of the expressed will of God without any thought of fighting back for restoration. Am I going too far in thinking that we can actually change God's mind—or does Scripture verify this conclusion?

In Exodus 32, God declares to Moses that He is going to destroy the nation of Israel. Not only that, He added, "I will make *you* into a great nation" (verse 10, NIV). What a temptation for Moses! God offered Moses an unusual opportunity to really become somebody.

Now the true intercessor in Moses emerges. Moses did not piously accept God's judgment as immutable. Nor did he give in to the temptation to replace Abraham as the father of faith and the father of a nation. Moses pleaded on behalf of his nation, reminding God of His own eternal purposes for Israel.

Then he prayed the boldest of all prayers. In effect, Moses said to God, "You can't destroy these people, and you cannot start over again with me. I know something about atonement. And I'm going to make atonement for the sins of these people. Here am I. Blot my name out from Your Book, which You have written."

Moses was not speaking in defiance of the Holy God, saying, "If you don't want Israel, then you can't have me either." No, he is ready to give himself up as the sacrifice of atonement. He is offering to do what Jesus did!

When we consider what he did, we see that he prayed with *insight* and with *authority*. He did not accept *a word from* the Lord as *the word of* the Lord. He was a man who did not just accept change, but one who caused change!

Moses spoke to God in such an impassioned manner that, hundreds of years later, God sent him from heaven (along with Elijah) to the Mount of Transfiguration. There Moses encouraged Jesus about the great intercession that He was about to accomplish in Jerusalem (see Luke 9:30–31). We must not forget to link Moses' ministry to Jesus on the Mount of Transfiguration to the event in Exodus 32 when his intercession turned God's anger to forgiveness.

His boldness is equalled only by the apostle Paul's who

prayed that, if it were possible, he might be damned in order that all Israel might be saved (see Romans 9:3).

Where are the intercessors today who will pray with passion? Where are the ones who are willing, if necessary, to complete in their own body the suffering of Jesus? (see Colossians 1:9, 24).

Throughout the centuries—and most sadly, today—Christians set a limit on their prayers. We do not trust enough in the love of God. We do not trust enough in His Word that we may come boldly before His throne of grace to present our petitions (see Hebrews 7:25).

Too few of us dare to become intercessors who will wrestle with God in prayer in an attempt to turn away His judgment. And so we have little idea of all that God means to accomplish in our world and in the lives of those we love.

How far are you willing to go as an intercessor in dealing with God? Do you trust in His love enough to do battle with Him?

Let the Lord Fight for You

H. David Edwards

Former president, Elim Bible
Institute; from Cocoa, Florida

Are you expecting God to fight your battles for you? Are you trying to fight His battles for Him? If your answer is yes to either question you are almost certainly facing defeat!

Before we explore this matter further there are three principles that I would like you to establish in your mind.

First, there are events on earth that involve the special concerns of heaven.

Second, when heaven's interests are involved, heaven's resources can be depended upon.

Third, when heaven's interests are involved, the outcome is not decided on earth but in heaven.

Bearing these principles in mind, when there is conflict and the issues at stake are of heavenly concern, then remember the words of 2 Chronicles 20:15, "The battle is not yours, but God's" (KJV).

I don't know what sort of battle or battles you might be facing, but I would like to suggest some things for you to evaluate.

Is the battle in which you find yourself one in which the

interests of heaven are at stake? If not, if the conflict is just between you and someone else and the issue does not involve the interests of heaven, then "make peace with thine enemy while thou art in the way with him." This is not the kind of battle to expect God to fight for you.

If, however, the battle is one in which the interests of heaven and the issues of eternity are at stake, then that is a different matter.

If you find yourself engaged in the Lord's battle, then it will not do to try and fight His battle for Him. Instead, commit the outcome to Him. So often we pray: "Now this, Father, is what I want You to do. I'm in a dilemma. I'm hemmed in on all sides, and it seems to me that if You were really my Father this is what You would now be doing. . . ." This is not really committing the issue to Him.

I have no way of knowing what He will do. There's no way for me to know how His ends are to be secured. But I can relax in the knowledge that "the battle is not mine but God's," if His interests are at stake. If it is His battle, then I can leave it alone. It is His reputation at stake and I can trust Him to do what is necessary to win His own victory.

King Jehoshaphat faced the combined forces of three nations and said to God, "We have no might against this great company that cometh against us; neither know we what to do: but our eyes are upon thee" (2 Chronicles 20:12, KJV).

As all Judah waited before the Lord the Holy Spirit came upon Jahaziel and he spoke the word of the Lord, saying, "Hearken ye, all Judah, and ye inhabitants of Jerusalem, and thou king Jehoshaphat, Thus saith the Lord unto you, Be not afraid nor dismayed by reason of this great multitude; for the battle is not yours, but God's" (verse 15).

It is significant, it seems to me, that Jahaziel did not say the *victory* is the Lord's, but the *battle* is the Lord's. In other words, "This isn't your fight, it's God's, and He'll take care of it Himself." So, it is not just we who are in conflict, but God Himself is involved in a conflict. In fact, God has, from the beginning, chosen to involve Himself in conflict.

Remember what the Lord said after Eve and Adam sinned?

He said, "I will put enmity. . . ." Not, I will succeed in victory, but I will establish conflict in the earth. In a very real sense, God started the fight! After that the issues were never between simply Canaan and Moab, or the Philistines and the Israelites, or Judah and Moab, or the children of Israel and the children of Amalek. The issue was and always is between God and the devil; the seed of God and the seed of Satan.

You may feel as the Israelites did at times when they lamented, "There is a mighty host against us." Might it be ignorance concerning the future? Inadequate financial resources? Uncertainty of the will of the Lord for your life? A divided household? Sickness?

Whatever it might be, identify it and declare honestly, "We have no might against this great host and we don't know what to do, but our eyes are upon Thee." Literally "throw up your hands" and throw that burden to Him—and don't take it back.

When we have established that the battle facing us is truly a battle between heaven and hell, then we can confidently join the hymn writer in singing:

> Then let my soul arise
> And tread the tempter down;
> My Captain leads me forth
> To conquest, and a crown.
> The feeblest saint
> Shall win the day,
> Though death and hell
> Obstruct the way.
>
> Isaac Watts

When heaven's interests can be recognized clearly in conflicts on earth, then heaven's resources can be counted on.

"For the battle is not yours, but God's." You can depend on it.

When Temptation Overwhelms You

Catherine Marshall

Founder of Breakthrough; author of fifteen books including *A Man Called Peter* and *Christy*

Knowing that His children would be buffeted constantly by temptation and attacks from Satan, God has provided for us a defense system through His Word, His response to our prayers and His light. Most of us have made good use of the first two, but how many of us know about the power of His light?

The Scripture base for this is Romans 13:12: "Let us therefore cast off the works of darkness, and let us put on the armour of light" (KJV). What this means is that as long as we stay in the light we are safe because Satan cannot endure light and will not come near it.

A housewife whom I'll call Mary discovered this one day at her point of urgent need. Her husband traveled a lot on business and occasionally on Sunday. Their neighbor and good friend, whom I'll call Ralph, went to the same church and offered Mary and her small daughter a ride to the Sunday service when her husband was out of town.

Nothing was wrong with that, except that soon it was becoming a habit. Mary found herself looking forward to seeing Ralph, she began to think of him often.

An inner warning signal went up for her as she remembered Jesus' words about lust beginning inside us—in the thoughts and will. "I'll duck this," she decided. She and her daughter went early to church to get there ahead of Ralph's proffered ride.

The strategy worked the first Sunday. But on the next one when her husband was out of town, Ralph started early for church, too, and picked them up.

On both sides the attraction was intensifying. Even sitting across the room from one another in a group of people, Mary was acutely conscious of Ralph and of his eyes often on her. An electric sexual attraction was developing between them, no question about it.

One night Mary forced herself to face the issue. "I made myself think through the end results if Ralph and I kept on the road we were going. A romantic interlude, nothing more? To think so would be kidding myself. Rather, probably a broken home. My husband's life cruelly hurt and twisted. Worse still for our child. And tawdriness as my reward. On the other side was the frightening intensity of the electricity between Ralph and me.

"In desperation, I dropped to my knees. 'O God! This is too much for me.' It was a cry wrung out of me. 'I can't fight anymore. I turn this battle over to You.' That night I slept calmly."

The next day with her husband still out of town, Mary spent the entire day cleaning closets, drawers, cupboards, windows. In some way, it must have been symbolic of the cleaning going on inside her.

That evening after her daughter was in bed, Ralph appeared at the front door. "My husband's not home," Mary told him. But he came in anyway.

Mary didn't ask her caller to sit down. She remained standing in the center of the room bathed in a cone of light from the electrical fixture overhead. There was an awkward interlude during which Ralph made persistent small talk, his eyes fastened on Mary. As she concentrated on Jesus as represented by that light, she felt herself becoming less aware of Ralph and more and more aware of the enveloping light of God all around her.

Finally her caller said he wanted to look at her sleeping daughter of whom he was very fond. Mary nodded, but did not follow him into the darkness of the adjoining bedroom. Somehow she knew that she must not. There in the darkness Ralph's arms would reach for her as inevitably as—no, *she must stay in the light*. As long as she stood in the light, the values she really cared about—her marriage, the home she and her husband had made together, their child—would be safe.

Ralph remained in the bedroom for what seemed like an eternity, waiting for her, Mary thought. At last he emerged. For a long moment he stood looking at Mary, indecision written on his face. At last, reluctantly, he left.

"Then I understood," Mary said later, "the truth of the teaching that there's nothing wrong with being tempted. It's what we do with the temptation that matters. My tumultuous feeling for Ralph did not disappear overnight. But as I prayed more about it, the entire episode just faded from my emotions, leaving no trauma, no scars, no regrets—just praise to God for delivering me from a serious temptation."

Mary had discovered for herself the reality of "the armour of light." That protecting armor is, of course, Jesus Himself as He prophesied in Isaiah's beautiful words:

> The people that walked in darkness have seen a great light: they that dwell in the land of the shadow of death, upon them hath the light shined.
>
> Isaiah 9:2, KJV

As His disciples, we are urged:

> For ye were sometimes darkness, but now are ye light in the Lord: walk as children of light.
>
> Ephesians 5:8, KJV

The Pulling Down of Strongholds

Is lust one of the strongholds in your life? Or is it envy? Or greed? Whatever has a grip on you, know that the Lord is ready to help you be freed. Hold on to this promise:

(For the weapons of our warfare are not carnal, but mighty through God to the pulling down of strongholds;) Casting down imaginations, and every high thing that exalteth itself against the knowledge of God, and bringing into captivity every thought to the obedience of Christ.

2 Corinthians 10:4–5, KJV

The picture comes to my mind of a strong, fortified castle-fortress atop a steep hill with precipitous cliffs all around. Deep inside a man or a woman is held in chains, a prisoner. The stronghold is guarded heavily. *This* is Satan's stronghold. The above passage tells us the weapons of our spiritual warfare are mighty and powerful to "pull down" and to demolish such strongholds.

But Scripture also tells us that Satan's strongholds are delusions, unreal, lies, just as everything he says is a lie and everything he tries to persuade us is real is not real at all. The only real Stronghold is Jesus Himself and the Truth that He is and stands for:

For You [Lord] have been a stronghold to the poor, a stronghold to the needy in his distress, a shelter from the storm, a shade from the heat; for the blast of the ruthless ones is like a rainstorm against a wall.

Isaiah 25:4, TAB

The Lord is good, a strength and stronghold in the day of trouble; He knows—recognizes, has knowledge of and understands—those who take refuge and trust in Him.

Nahum 1:7, TAB

Our refuge—no matter what the temptation—is in the light of Jesus' presence. There He shows us His truth and there He keeps us from stumbling into Satan's lair.

A Warrior's Prayer

Victor M. Matthews

I am grateful, heavenly Father, that the Lord Jesus Christ triumphed over all principalities and dark powers. I claim that victory for my life today. I reject all the accusations and temptations of Satan. I affirm that the Word of God is true and I choose to live today in the light of His Word. Open my eyes and show me the areas of my life that do not please You. Work in me to cleanse me from all ground that would give Satan a foothold against me.

I am thankful that You have made a provision so that today I can live filled with the Spirit of God, with love and joy and peace, with long-suffering, gentleness and goodness, with meekness, faithfulness and self-control in my life. I recognize that this is Your will for me and so I reject and resist all the endeavors of Satan and his wicked spirits to rob me of the will of God.

In my own life today I tear down the strongholds of Satan and smash the plans of Satan that have been formed against me. I tear down the strongholds of Satan against my mind, and I surrender my mind to You, blessed Holy Spirit. I affirm, heavenly Father, that You have not given me the spirit of fear, but of power and of love and of a sound mind. I break and smash the strongholds of Satan formed against my emotions today and I give my emotions to You. I smash the strongholds of Satan formed against my will today, I give my will to You and choose to make the right decisions of faith. I smash the strongholds of Satan formed against my body today. I give my body to You recognizing that I am Your temple. I rejoice in Your mercy and goodness.

Heavenly Father, I pray that now and through this day You would strengthen and enlighten me, show me the way Satan is hindering and tempting and lying and distorting the truth in my life.

I cover myself with the blood of the Lord Jesus Christ and pray that You, blessed Holy Spirit, would bring all the work of the crucifixion, all the work of the resurrection, all the work of the glorification and all the work of Pentecost into my life today.

Amen

Esther: A Courageous Lady

Derek Prince

Ministers worldwide; author of more than thirty books; from Ft. Lauderdale, Florida

Though today's news is dominated by the actions of presidents, kings and governments, it is my conviction that our world is ruled by those people *who know how to pray*.

Looking back through history, I see the ministry of intercession as God's method of answering problems that cannot be resolved in any other way. Thus intercession is truly one of the highest ministries open to any Christian.

Some intercessors will work quietly behind the scenes, yet exercise with power a gift God has given them. Then there are those who are called to intercede—or stand in the gap—for people or causes. Moses, for example, was constantly standing between God and His chosen people, pleading for them. Abraham did this for Sodom and Gomorrah. Such intercessors are especially close to the heart of God.

Queen Esther was also one of these intercessors. Her Old Testament story has much to teach us about the faith that is needed for this kind of intercession. Esther was a lovely Jewish maiden in the Persian Empire at the time of the exile of her people from Israel. She was an orphan, who had been brought up by her uncle, Mordecai, an important official in the court of the Persian emperor.

Because she was not only beautiful in looks, but also in spirit, Esther had been chosen to be Queen of the Persian Empire, a position of tremendous influence and importance in the emperor's palace. At Mordecai's insistence, however, Esther had never publicly revealed the fact that she was Jewish.

After she became queen, a certain anti-semitic official named Haman tricked the emperor into signing a decree that would put to death all the Jews in Persia on the false grounds that they were disobeying all the emperor's laws. The plan, if carried out, would result in total destruction of the entire Jewish nation.

When this decree went forth, Mordecai sent a message to Esther in the queen's palace, that it was her responsibility to persuade the King to change his mind about the decree.

Esther's reply:

> "For any man or woman who approaches the king in the inner court without being summoned the king has but one law: that he be put to death. The only exception to this is for the king to extend the gold scepter to him and spare his life. But thirty days have passed since I was called to go to the king."
>
> Esther 4:11, NIV

Mordecai sent back this answer:

> "Do not think that because you are in the king's house you alone of all the Jews will escape. For if you remain silent at this time, relief and deliverance for the Jews will arise from another place, but you and your father's family will perish. And who knows but that you have come to royal position for such a time as this?"
>
> Verses 12–14

Then Esther sent this reply to Mordecai:

> "Go, gather together all the Jews who are in Susa, and fast for me. Do not eat or drink for three days,

night or day. I and my maids will fast as you do. When this is done, I will go to the king, even though it is against the law. And if I perish, I perish."

So Mordecai went away and carried out all of Esther's instructions.

Verses 16–17

What a picture of an intercessor! Note the commitment—"If I perish, I perish." Whether Esther lived or died was not the most important question, but what she could do for her people.

Esther also knew that there are times when praying, alone, is not enough, thus she asked her people to fast three days and three nights.

Imagine her tension when she went to the palace three days later and stood in the inner court, facing the King's hall. How would he respond? Was she going to her death?

When the King saw Queen Esther, he was pleased with her and held out to her the gold scepter that was in his hand. Then he asked her, "What is your request, Queen Esther? Even up to half the kingdom, it will be given you."

At this point victory was won for the Jewish people. It is always won, I believe, through intercession. When Esther then boldly revealed to the king Haman's plot to destroy her people, Haman was put to death and his palace given to Queen Esther.

Note this beautiful fact about Esther. When she went to the king, she didn't go as a beggar, she didn't grovel, she put on her royal robes. She stood there in his presence, a lovely queen. She took her rightful position.

I believe the same applies to you and me as Christians. We're to recognize who we are in God's sight—the position that God has elevated us to. We are not to grovel. We are not to go as beggars. In one sense, these words from Isaiah describe Esther:

Awake, awake, O Zion, clothe yourself with strength. Put on your garments of splendor, O Jerusalem, the holy city. The uncircumcised and defiled will not enter you again. Shake off your dust; rise up, sit en-

throned, O Jerusalem. Free yourself from the chains
on your neck, O captive Daughter of Zion.

Isaiah 52:1–2, NIV

Those men and women who are mature in intercession have
the following:

1. Intimacy with God.
2. Boldness in approaching God.
3. Conviction of God's absolute justice, both positive and negative, that God will spare the righteous but judge the wicked.
4. A concern for God's glory and, conversely, a disregard of personal interests and ambition.
5. A dedication to the task, even at the cost of life itself.
6. Willingness to identify with those for whom we intercede.

VI
Scriptural Praying

As an intercessor you need one essential tool—the Holy Bible. You will find its wealth inexhaustible. In it somewhere are answers to every question you will ever have.

Keep the Bible handy as you pray. Ask God to place in your mind those verses of Scripture that will help the person for whom you are praying. The more verses of Scripture you know, the more help you can offer to hurting people.

Keeping a journal as you pray is also valuable. When the Lord gives you a word or an order or a direction to take, then you can write it down.

You and your Bible should become inseparable.

How Scripture Strengthens Personal Prayer

Edith Marshall

Christian counselor; from Orleans, Massachusetts

Several months after my husband, Peter, had accepted the pastorate of our second church and we had moved to the picturesque village of East Dennis on Cape Cod, I was invited to come and pick raspberries in the backyard of one of the wisest and dearest men I have ever known. He was the Rev. John Stanton, retired Presbyterian minister.

Carrying my berry-picking basket, I wandered up the crushed-shell driveway beside a rambling, weathered shingle house. He was sitting in the backyard, a huge Bible in his lap, his eyes closed, his lips moving. I knew he must be praying—except for the fact that every once in a while his eyes would open to focus on his Bible, only to be shut tight in a few seconds.

In a few moments he spotted me out of the corner of his eye, and beckoned me over with a warm welcome.

"I don't mean to interrupt," I apologized.

"Oh," he chuckled, "I'm praying my way through the Psalms. It's marvelous!"

As I looked puzzled, he explained that because so many of

the Psalms are addressed to the Lord, they lend themselves to being incorporated into our own personal prayer lives and that he was simply personalizing them as his own prayer. His prayers were rich as a result—full of praise and thanksgiving. And since his supplications were prayed according to the will of God, he had the assurance his prayers would be answered.

But not wanting to seem super-spiritual, he showed me to the berry patch and set me to work.

Since my prayer life seemed dull at the time, I determined to try Dr. John's approach. The very next morning, with my Bible opened in front of me, I began praying out loud the passages that lent themselves to prayer.

Some Psalms needed no paraphrasing to become my own heartfelt prayer:

> Create in me a clean heart, O God, and put a new and right spirit within me. Cast me not away from thy presence, and take not thy holy Spirit from me. Restore to me the joy of thy salvation, and uphold me with a willing spirit.
>
> Psalm 51:10–12, RSV

Others could be made my own prayers by switching some wording:

> Lord, You are my shepherd. When You're there I have no needs. You make me still in the inner man and give me peace. You lift up, restore and heal my soul. Please lead me in Your paths of righteousness for Your name's sake. . . .
>
> Psalm 23

On my next visit to Dr. John's, I shared with him my new-found enthusiasm for praying the Psalms. And I added that certain passages in the New Testament also pointed up my needs. For example:

O Lord, let me live by the Spirit and walk by the
Spirit. Free me from self-conceit. Let there be in me
no provoking of another and no envy.

Galatians 5:25

Or if there was something I didn't understand:

Lord, how can I work out my salvation with fear and
trembling? Is there something I must do, or something to repent of? Show me, Lord!

Philippians 2:12

Dr. John confirmed my experiences thus far, and then taught
me about using the Scriptures to intercede for others.

"Do the same things you've been doing in praying for yourself," he said. "But now put the other person's name in the
Scripture passage wherever it's needed."

I could do this in the following way:

O Lord, You who have begun a good work (in Ellen)
. . . bring it to completion (in her).

Philippians 1:6

Or:

Blessed be the Lord who daily bears (Ellen) up. God
is (her) salvation. Our God is a God of salvation, and
to God, the Lord, belongs escape from death.

Psalm 68:19–20

I found that on nearly every page of the Bible there was a
phrase or a sentence that I could turn into a prayer for someone
else. There were also Scriptures with promises I could claim for
others that could be turned into prayers:

O Lord, as (Ellen) passes through the waters and
rivers, be with her, that they not overflow (her). Keep
her from being burned by the fire.

Isaiah 43:2

As (Ellen) walks through this affliction, work in her a far more exceeding and eternal weight of glory.

2 Corinthians 4:17

Another example:

Cause (Ellen) to wait for You that (her) strength might be renewed. Then (she) can mount up with wings like eagles, (she) can run and not be weary, (she) can walk and not faint.

Isaiah 40:31

What a wealth of resource and inspiration for prayer is available when we but open His Word!

What Can Happen When You Pray God's Word

Leonard LeSourd

Chairman of Breakthrough; former editor, *Guideposts* magazine; associate publisher, Chosen Books; from Lincoln, Virginia

For many years I watched Catherine disappear in the early morning to be alone with God. It was a time during our devotional period in which we separated for half an hour to read and pray and listen. There in her office she would kneel in front of her upholstered chair, Bible open in front of her.

"What is Your Word for Ginny?" she might pray, concerned over a friend's failing marriage. Often a verse would come to mind, or a Psalm. Sometimes a whole chapter of the Bible. She would turn the pages quickly. The passage reached might have an answer or be a clue to another verse that might be helpful.

If she was deeply upset about something or someone, Catherine would clutch the Bible fiercely, beseeching heaven for help, saying in effect: "Lord, You have the answer right here in Your Word. I just know You do."

If no passage came to mind, she would open her Bible at random and read, then pray, then read, then pray some more until an answer came. Sometimes it took hours.

This type of Scripture prayer nourished Catherine. I could

tell how much of a cherished time it was by the excited look in her eyes when she returned to our bedroom.

What is Scripture praying? It is a form of prayer that many of us practice, perhaps instinctively, without giving it a name. Some refer to it as *praying God's Word*.

Thirty years ago when my world seemed to be falling apart, I found myself repeating the Twenty-Third Psalm over and over: "The Lord is my shepherd, I shall not want. . . ." I didn't exactly think of it as a prayer at the time, but of course it was . . . a desperate call for help. The Scripture words were a balm to my spirit. The Lord truly became my shepherd.

A mother concerned about her son's errant lifestyle said her prayer this way:

> Jerry, the Lord is thy Shepherd, thou shalt not want. . . . He leadeth thee in the paths of righteousness. . . .

Repeating the words from many of the Psalms can be effective prayers. Try it this way for a friend you want to resist temptation:

> Blessed is (Gary) who walketh not in the counsel of the ungodly. (Gary's) delight is in the law of the Lord. (Gary) shall be like a tree planted by the rivers of water.
>
> Psalm 1:1–3

Or try it this way for the wife you want to remain pure:

> (Lisa) is far more precious than jewels. . . . The heart of (Lisa's) husband trusts her. . . . (*Lisa*) does him good, and not harm all the days of her life. . . .
>
> Proverbs 31:10–12

What comes out of Scripture prayer is not only a deeper knowledge of the Bible, but a more intimate relationship with God. *He is there with you.* Would it surprise you to learn that we minister to the Lord as we pray His Word back to Him? (See Proverbs 15:8.)

With the millions of believers now arising early in the morning for one- to two-hour prayer sessions, either alone or in groups, Scripture praying is becoming more and more common. At a conference outside St. Louis a few years ago, a group of us got up each morning to pray from 5 A.M. to 7 A.M. We came armed with Bibles. Scripture readings not only refreshed us, they guided our prayers into new areas. Petitions for personal concerns soon became intercession for our leaders, nations and even for our adversaries.

What I learned during my prayer times is that if I try to pray quietly for a lengthy period, I often run out of people and situations to pray for. Then can come restlessness, tiredness, even boredom. *But the Word anoints the prayers.* The Word somehow releases the Holy Spirit to supply extra power in prayer.

Another method of scriptural prayer is to take a meaningful passage and let God teach its deeper meanings. Try, for example, the story of the woman caught in adultery (John 8:2–11). First, read it through and ask God to reveal what His teaching is for you in these verses.

Next, read the words again slowly, prayerfully. Linger on those words that seem meant for you. Do you identify with the accusers? The sinner? Both? Neither?

Then listen. What is God saying? Let yourself be like a child nestled in God's lap, listening to His words.

Last, *let Him take over.* Let Him love you. Let Him console you. Let Him forgive you.

This kind of prayer gets you out of the way so that God's Word can edify you, heal you, restoring you to the person He wants you to be.

Jesus, Our Intercessor

Sondra Johnson

Communications director, Breakthrough; administrator, Christian Guidance and Counseling
Center; from Hillsboro, Virginia

Because Jesus is our primary Intercessor, I began one day to comb the Bible for everything He had to say on the subject, hoping to learn the kinds of things He prayed for. Instead, I was struck more by "how" he prayed. Only once, for example, did He ask for something for Himself: "Father, if Thou art willing, remove this cup from Me (Luke 22:42, NAS).

But even then, at a time when He was in agony and His sweat became like great clots of blood dropping down upon the ground (Luke 22:44), He still had the courage to add, "Yet not my will, but always yours, be done" (NIV).

The Lord's Prayer (Matthew 6:9–13) is the most familiar of Christ's prayers. But the type of prayer most often referred to in the Bible is that of Jesus giving thanks, usually before food and drink (Luke 24:30).

Jesus seemed to prefer to pray alone:

> And after He had dismissed the multitude, He went
> up into the hills by Himself to pray. When it was
> evening He was still there alone.
>
> Matthew 14:23, TAB

> And in the early morning, while it was still dark, He arose and went out and departed to a lonely place, and was praying there.
>
> Mark 1:35, NAS

> But He Himself would often slip away to the wilderness and pray.
>
> Luke 5:16, NAS

Jesus warns us to pray, especially that we will be worthy to escape all things that will take place before we meet the Son of Man (Luke 21:36).

There seemed to be great emotion, often joy, in Jesus' conversations with His Father:

> In that same hour He rejoiced and glorifed in the Holy Spirit and said, I thank You, Father, Lord of heaven and earth, that You have concealed these things [relating to salvation] from the wise and understanding and learned, and revealed them to babes—the childish, unskilled and untaught. Yes, Father, for such was Your gracious will and choice and good pleasure.
>
> Luke 10:21, TAB

> "Father, I thank Thee that Thou heardest Me."
>
> John 11:41, NAS

There was seldom any change in attitude or countenance when Jesus began to pray. He would simply turn His conversation from one of His friends to His Father, much as any of us might do when having a family discussion.

As I have found a special joy in spending long hours talking with a close and trusted friend, so, too, did Jesus with His Father:

> And it was at this time that He went off to the mountain to pray, and He spent the whole night in prayer to God.
>
> Luke 6:12, NAS

Jesus' prayers contained easy-to-understand words coming right from His heart, often expressing great pain:

> But Jesus was saying, "Father forgive them; for they do not know what they are doing."
>
> Luke 23:34, NAS

> My God, My God, why have You abandoned Me— leaving Me helpless, forsaking and failing Me in My need?
>
> Matthew 27:46, TAB

During an entire chapter of John, we are privileged to have Jesus' long conversation with God, almost a wrap-up of His life on earth. And as He prayed for safety, salvation and love for His disciples, He remembered us—those who were to come after the disciples—even in His great distress (John 17:20).

My probings into *how* Jesus prayed brought me to these four conclusions:

1. Prayer should be a simple and direct communication between the one praying and our Father in heaven (Matthew 6:5–13).
2. Prayer should be done relentlessly and in perfect faith (Matthew 7:7–8; Luke 11:9, 13).
3. Prayer is intended to help us avoid temptation (Matthew 26:41).
4. Prayer must be done with a forgiving and humble heart (Mark 11:24–26; Luke 18:10–14).

I was also reminded that where two or more are gathered in prayer, there must be agreement (Matthew 18:19–20) and that we must pray for those who curse and abuse us (Luke 6:28).

After going over my notes, one thing stood out with painful clarity: It is not my words that matter in prayer, but my *attitude*. Jesus, who left us a perfect example of how to live, also showed us how to reach God in prayer, allowing us to tap the only real Source of power there is!

The Penny Prayer

Elizabeth Sherrill

Author of *Journey Into Rest*; co-author of many books including *The Hiding Place*; from Westchester County, New York

Before going to sleep that Monday night, I had a promise to keep. As he left on a business trip, my husband, John, had asked for prayer, both that evening and the following day. My first step was to reach for my bedside Bible. Whenever I tried to pray without Scripture to keep my focus on God, my thoughts invariably bogged down on the problems—and there were plenty of them in the current situation.

Earlier that day John had flown out to Grand Rapids, Michigan, where the next day—Tuesday, September 6, 1982—he would take part in merger talks between our small publishing company and a large corporation. But what about the particular kind of Christian publishing we believed God had called us to? Could it survive such a merger? And what about our small staff?

"Pray!" John had said as he left for the airport. And so I opened the Bible and once again watched the familiar phenomenon take place: My thoughts were channeled by Scripture away from mere worry into authentic intercession.

The decisive meeting, out in Michigan, was to begin the following day at two o'clock. That was the hour when John and our partner Len LeSourd would be sitting down with the officers of the corporation.

As it happened I, too, had a trip scheduled on Tuesday, a drive of 150 miles through upstate New York. It was a beautiful early autumn day and my route was a spectacular one through the Catskill Mountains. About noon I passed an irresistible wooden signpost: "Escarpment Trail."

I backed the car into the pull-off and set out on foot up the mountainside. The path climbed through a pine and oak forest so silent and splendid that by the time I looked at my watch it was already two o'clock, the hour I had assured John I would be remembering him and Len in Grand Rapids. About a hundred yards from the trail I spotted an outcropping of rock. I worked my way to it through the branches, sat down and closed my eyes.

All that came in the whispering silence beneath the pines was a string of self-accusations. Maybe God had never wanted us to go into publishing in the first place. Or maybe He had—still did. Maybe this merger idea was only our own wishful way out of the cashflow problems created by the recession.

I knew, of course, that this kind of fretting was not prayer. But my Bible, which could have given me perspective, was in the car miles away at the foot of the mountain. How could I stop my mind from running in problem-centered circles? How could I really, meaningfully, hold up the men meeting in Grand Rapids?

I opened my eyes. And blinked.

On the ground, not two feet away, lay a bright copper penny. I reached down and picked it up. How a shiny new coin came to be lying on that remote mountain slope I could not imagine. I sat staring at it as though it were the first penny I had ever seen.

Lincoln's profile . . . arching over his head the words *IN GOD WE TRUST* . . . below, *1982* . . . and the word *LIBERTY*.

Why—I wasn't holding just a penny! Here were the themes for my prayer.

In God we trust. Not in our skill at negotiating. What books we were to publish, the welfare of other people, God knew the answers! "This afternoon in Grand Rapids, Father, let Len and John take a new step in trusting You."

1982. He wasn't the God of a distant past or an imaginary future; He was God of the present moment. "Father, show Len and John Your will, this year, for this situation."

Liberty. Freedom for those in prison—of any and every kind—was always the will of God. "Father, release Len and John to use the skills You've given them—to work with words and not with numbers."

And those whose skills were different, those with God's gifts of business management and marketing: "Father, let the decisions in Grand Rapids mean new liberty for them as well!"

God. Trust. Liberty. My penny prayer went on so long that I became conscious of the hard rock beneath me. Three words in Latin on the reverse side of the coin caught my attention as I stood up. *E PLURIBUS UNUM: "out of many, one."* Was God telling me with a chuckle that the merger *was* His answer, that out of these two companies, one was to emerge?

That was, as it turned out, the result of the deliberations that afternoon in Grand Rapids. The merger was completed in 1982, a merger that encouraged us to pursue our particular philosophy of publishing and allowed God to show His faithfulness in caring for the needs of the staff.

I did not know this as I hiked back down the mountain that September afternoon with a penny in my pocket. I only knew I had a secret to intercession, anywhere I found myself. God has filled the world with clues to His presence; the humblest object can remind us that He is in charge.

VII
Igniting the
Church

If you belong to a church that does not have a specific ministry of intercession, tell your pastor that he is operating with only a fraction of the power his church could have.

Pastors desperately need intercessors praying for them during this era of all-out spiritual warfare. When a team of prayer warriors goes to work in a church, it can truly become a power center, not only for the church, but the whole community.

Love on Its Knees

Dick Eastman

President, Every Home for Christ; author; from Chatsworth, California

In 1971 Pastor Dick Eastman was called by the Lord to mobilize an army of intercessors to impact the world for the Kingdom of God. Here is the "story behind the story" of a venture that has impacted more than a million lives in 120 countries.

It began in the late 1960s. I set up a retreat in the nearby Sierra Nevada Mountains for 22 teenagers in our church. None of us was experienced in prolonged prayer sessions, certainly not for an entire night.

We were ready to give up after an hour. Then the youngest boy there, a thirteen-year-old, had a suggestion. "Why don't we start praying in a different way—as warriors?"

Then, with tears in his eyes, he described how he saw himself and his friends as warring against the darkness of the booze-sex-drugs lifestyle of the hippie communes that had sprung up all across southern California. He asked us to stand with him all night to "fight the devil."

By three in the morning, a spirit of brokenness had settled over our retreat house. The room was warmly lit by a glow from logs burning in a large fireplace, but also from a fire burning within the young people themselves. We all began to weep and cry out. One seventeen-year-old student lay on her face in the middle of the room weeping for the youth of California who were in trouble with drugs.

I was witnessing what our forebears used to call a "spirit of travail," a wonderful word related to the word *work* or *labor*, as in giving birth. (See Romans 8:26–27.)

This was the beginning. Soon intercessory retreats from our church began to flourish, until 175 young people were participating. Within a year the Jesus Movement began in many parts of California. At least 800,000 young people would find Christ in those same exciting days.

It was in a motel room beside Lake Michigan that God gave me further insight regarding His army of intercessors. One morning there I had come to the final chapters of the book of Revelation and, pausing to meditate on the literal nature of the Lamb's Book of Life, I suddenly found myself longing to pray about names *yet to be added* to these celestial records.

"Lord, please let me participate in a movement that adds more names to the Book of Life than have been added in all of history," I prayed.

It was a bold prayer, indeed, but somehow I felt the Holy Spirit had led me to say the words. Tears began to flow as I stood up and walked to the window of my motel room.

Before me was the vast expanse of Lake Michigan lying placidly like a giant sheet of glass. As the sun's rays sparkled off the lake I saw millions of tiny diamond-like bursts of light dancing in the distance. It reminded me of the description in Revelation of the multitude of redeemed humanity who will someday stand upon a sheet of glass (Revelation 15:2). Then I recalled the promise of how "blood-washed" souls would come out of every kindred, tongue, people and nation (Revelation 5:9). I wondered if God had chosen this moment to reveal to me the role of intercessors in global evangelism.

Lifting my face in anticipation, I experienced a second vision.

Before me, in a large arena, stood a multitude representing every age group. I sensed they were committed intercessors.

Each held a page containing names. Then my attention was drawn in the opposite direction. There I saw a throne and an angel who held a huge book. As I watched, each intercessor came to the throne and presented his or her list of names.

One of those individuals caught my particular attention. Although her face was wrinkled and her hair gray, she beamed with the joy of Jesus. I asked the Lord what all this meant.

These are the names of souls these warriors helped bring to salvation.

"Where did the intercessors get these names?" I asked.

Come, and I will show you, came the answer.

With that I saw this joyous elderly saint, on her knees, flying swiftly through the heavenlies. It was a strange sight. In my spirit I knew that she was flying thousands of miles. In an instant, she descended to a village, in Asia, perhaps, or India. My attention was drawn to a hut that appeared to be the focus of the saint's intercession.

The hut was modest, even by the standards of the village. Within were a small table, a chair and a bed. Its lone occupant was a middle-aged man who appeared to be of Indian descent, most likely a Hindu.

As the intercessor continued in prayer above the hut, I noticed that even with the sun shining brightly, the hut was dark.

Then I noticed movement in the village. A man was distributing Gospel literature. He paused at the hut and knocked. When the occupant opened the door the worker handed him a Gospel booklet.

Through all this the elderly saint remained stationary in the heavenlies as if waiting for something.

Closing the door, the Hindu read a few sentences that told him about a loving heavenly Father who came to earth in the form of a Man, God's only Son. This concept was beyond the Hindu's comprehension since he believed there were many gods. A monkey could be a god, or a cow, or snake. "One God, one Son," he said. "Nonsense." He tossed the book on the table. The darkness of the room seemed to prevent his comprehension of the truth.

The man's rejection of the message was the cue for the intercessor. Through the roof of the hut she plunged, landing on her knees. The Hindu, of course, had no idea she was there.

Reaching her hands forward along the floor, with her palms up, the elderly woman appeared to be lifting something. Then I realized what she was doing. She was lifting the darkness in the room! The more she prayed, the more the darkness moved. When she had raised it high enough, she slowly moved from her knees and began pushing the darkness toward the ceiling from a crouched position, a few inches at a time, as she continued her intercessions. Before long she had pushed the darkness above the man, warring all the while against the satanic forces.

The instant the darkness rose above the man's head, he turned again toward the table, gazing intently upon the message he had earlier rejected. Now there was a different look on his face, a look of longing.

As he took the booklet into his hand, I could hear his thoughts. *Perhaps I was hasty in rejecting this message,* he reasoned. As he read again the claims of Christ, an amazing thing happened. He lifted his face toward heaven, his unseen praying guest contending against the darkness above him, and he cried out to the Lord, "I believe You are the Son of God!"

Joy flooded the faces of both the new convert and the elderly intercessor. A miracle was happening before my eyes. In that instant a brilliant beam of light penetrated the hut and flowed into the heart of the new believer. He had seen the Light— literally.

Stepping from the hut, still unseen by the rejoicing Indian, the intercessor pulled a piece of paper from her pocket. It was the list she had presented to the angel with the book. The happy warrior added the man's name to her long list. Then, with a shout of praise, she tucked the list back into her pocket and headed for a hut across the way.

For the next several minutes I sat in my motel room, wondering quietly about the strange picture I had just witnessed. Had my imagination run wild or had I truly observed an intercessor in action? Any vision must find confirmation in God's Word.

Almost immediately I was led to this passage regarding the power of God's light to penetrate the darkness:

> "Arise, shine, for your light has come, and the glory of the Lord rises upon you. See . . . thick darkness is over the peoples, but the Lord rises upon you and his glory appears over you. Nations will come to your light, and kings to the brightness of your dawn.
>
> "Lift up your eyes and look about you: All assemble and come to you; your sons come from afar, and your daughters are carried on the arm. Then you will look and be radiant, your heart will throb and swell with joy; the wealth on the seas will be brought to you, to you the riches of the nations will come."
>
> Isaiah 60:1–5, NIV

How God Dealt with a Successful (But Complacent) Church

Jim Croft

Pastor, Gold Coast Christian Cathedral; author; from Boca Raton, Florida

A year ago our leaders felt that if the 450 people of our church were to have any new visitation from God, there had to be church-wide fasting, intercession and repentance. So we chose a 21-day period and announced it to the membership.

We did not enter the fast with the proper attitude. The first problem was that things were going too well for us. Church finances were up considerably. Worship was good. New members were being added regularly.

Secondly, we were not novices to prayer and fasting. Dr. Derek Prince, one of our ruling elders, had written two books on prayer and fasting and was instrumental in founding Intercessors for America. Others in the leadership had been deeply involved in this kind of ministry. Also, our church has had a continued nightly prayer watch, operating eight hours per night, 365 days per year, since 1977.

Yet we were to discover we had a prideful view of our maturity and wisdom in prayer.

About twelve people came for prayer the first morning. By the third day it had dwindled to about four. Even our leaders showed little interest. Then the Lord began to speak to one of our lay leaders, Art Maki, that this fact was not the work of man, but was ordained by God Himself. The Lord insisted to him that at least a tithe, or a tenth, of the congregation of 450 appear before Him every morning. That night Art expressed his heart at our midweek service.

The fourth morning we had more than forty come out; by the sixth day, more than sixty. That morning God began to move us to confess and repent of uncharitable attitudes and murmurings toward the leadership, as well as one another. This was only the beginning of a period of heartrending repentance. The Lord made it abundantly clear that we had an appointment with Him early each morning. On the eighth day, God told us through prophecy that this visitation was like Halley's comet. Should we fail to make the effort to seek it out, it would not appear again during our lifetime.

The leadership and people awakened from their worldly stupor and hearkened to the voice of the Lord. By the tenth day, more than 240 persons came out, many bringing their small children. It was a glorious sight to see toddlers slumbering peacefully as their parents sought God in the early hours. The attendance remained well over 200 daily for the remainder of the 21 days. Frankly most of us were frightened not to attend because God was moving to such a depth that we did not want to miss a thing.

Perhaps the biggest surprise to us was that the Lord held us in a posture of soul-shaking repentance for fifteen days. We initially scheduled a brief time for repentance, presuming that it was a formality rather than a genuine need. Like many other Spirit-filled, Bible-believing churches, we did not fathom the gravity of our spiritual condition or the depth of repentance and cleansing that was needed. We imagined the repentance to be expressing sorrow for personal inconsistencies and a few national sins, such as abortion and pornography.

But like the Laodicean church, we needed the Holy Spirit's eye salve so that we could begin to comprehend our true spiritual condition. We needed to discern that we had backslidden due to our compromise with the world. We were rapidly losing our distinctiveness as the salt of the earth (Matthew 5:13). For five days we attempted to empty ourselves of all hidden sin at the personal level, but we still experienced a sense of uncleanness.

Then the fear of God began to come upon us. Our spiritual self-sufficiency began to dissipate. Two hundred-plus adults began to prostrate themselves with faces on the floor for an hour or more. Few had the courage to pray aloud. There was a wounded, bleeding Lamb tiptoeing among us, inspecting every facet of our lives. The Holy Spirit revealed that repentance is a gift as real as the gifts of salvation and healing. If He did not gift us with the ability to repent, we would be stuck in the mire of our own superficiality and worldly remorse.

It became apparent that we all, to varying degrees, had been guilty of frustrating the grace of God in our lives. Many repented of transgressions because they could see them hindering God's blessings. The Spirit brought on wave after wave of contrition and tears over offenses that we had considered minor, like misuse of time through over-indulgences in TV.

On several occasions, people repented of moral improprieties such as abortions, fornication and adultery, confessing them to leaders stationed at various places in the sanctuary. It was deeply moving to see the sweet joy of salvation return to friends who had been secretly bound for years.

The Spirit also began to uncover numerous ways our church had offended Him. We were guilty of pride, unfriendliness and self-centeredness. We had not exemplified His heart toward the lost, backslidden, wounded and oppressed.

I confessed that we leaders had been extravagant with our travel and entertainment expenses. We also tended to purchase more spiritual resource material than we could ever possibly use. We also confessed the sins of churches and ministries throughout the nation that have been manipulative and extravagant with finances.

Other burdens God led us to repent for:

1. The rising divorce rate among Christians, and the slaughter of millions of babies through abortion. (Many wept as

though they had personally argued the divorce case or performed the abortions.)
2. Not giving Jesus His due headship and preeminence.
3. Slighting the Holy Spirit by trying to use Him as an errand boy.
4. Our lack of unity and not loving one another.
5. Not fulfilling the Great Commission.
6. Not caring for the weak and helpless.
7. Despising and mistreating the Jewish people through the centuries.
8. Compromising with and becoming defiled by the spirit of the world.

On the fifteenth day, God allowed us to get past repentance. He gave us a new appreciation for the blood of Jesus and the indescribable agony that Christ endured to pay for our sins. Subsequently, as I have pondered why the Lord held us in repentance so long, Luke 7:47 has come to mind: Those who know they have been forgiven much have a capacity to love the Lord with more devotion than those who have been forgiven little.

Results! We had torn down walls of alienation as we labored together in the spirit of intercession. We had a new sense of intimacy, belonging and spiritual family. We knew by the witness of the Spirit those who were expressing the Lord's mind, not by their spiritual knowledge or fervency, but rather by the inner amens. Any prayers not from the mind of Christ were instantly recognized as such, even though they were laced with Scripture and good intentions.

Curiously, during the whole 21 days, not one prayer was uttered for personal needs. God directed us to utilize our faith for the deeper needs of His Body. Though it is legitimate to pray and fast for personal provision such as health, prosperity and guidance (Isaiah 58), we found ourselves joyfully apprehending repentance, cleansing and unity for the church through faith.

Nonetheless, a number of marriages were healed, and there were physical healings. I, for one, have labored with hypertension for several years. My blood pressure was 135/96. In the midst of our repentance I was happily at 118/80. Since that time it has stayed well within normal range.

The fast has been over for months, but the afterglow is spiritually invigorating. Many still come every morning to meet the Lord and harmonize in touching God on behalf of one another and furtherance of the Kingdom.

What is God saying to the Western church today? For the past year God has led hundreds of churches and thousands of believers around the world into a life-changing boot camp of early morning prayer and fasting. Repentance usually follows. This is what God has on the agenda for every church willing to help pave the way for the next wave of the Spirit of God.

The Need for Watering Holes

Margaret Therkelsen

Teacher and prayer group leader; from Lexington, Kentucky

In the old West nothing was more soothing to the cowboy than the distant view of stately cottonwood trees. They usually signified that close by was a watering hole, that stream of fresh, flowing water to quench the thirst and allow a few moments of rest and refreshment for the cowboy and his horse. Often these watering holes would be places where other cowboys would gather to push back the loneliness of the frontier and provide companionship.

God has spoken to us here that He needs "watering holes" today, where thirsty people can be refreshed and encouraged to deepen their commitment to Jesus and His Kingdom. We believe that the prayer group movement is part of the watering-hole system of God for this present age. We believe such groups are a necessity for developing holy habits of prayer and intercession, for helping the Body of Christ learn to love one another and for stretching our hearts and minds to take on the tasks God has for us.

The prayer group to which I belong has been meeting at our church about two and a half years. We have found there are three basic requirements for long-range participation. First and foremost, a serious *commitment to attendance* each Tuesday night. In our determination to reverence the use of time in each other's lives, we begin promptly at 7:00 and pray until 8:30. When the Spirit of prayer is strong and compelling, we have continued for an additional half hour. But we feel a sense of responsibility to be prompt in our prayer time. The Holy Spirit has led us into extended times of individual ministry in homes.

The second requirement has been *confidentiality*. We have covenanted to keep our prayer requests and personal sharings strictly within the group. As we have grown from several to 35 to 45 women, this is still a basic premise of the group. We honor the covenant of privacy.

Third, there is a seriousness of *intent to go all the way with God in our prayer life.* This God-given intention started with several women and is now permeating all our younger women with a winsomeness that only God can produce. We are finding that God the Holy Spirit builds a huge thirst in our desires and motivations to know Him better, and the weekly coming to the watering hole acts as an encouragement, an affirmation and a thrilling challenge.

After the first year, our attendance, which was running between eight and fifteen, suddenly opened up into a great inrush of women, which forced us to view the group differently. No longer was it a small, intimate setting where everyone was personally known, but it blossomed into a group of people we did not know, from many denominations. It was no longer a place to voice just our intimate concerns, but instead we felt that God had "taken over" for His divine purposes.

This change was a challenge to us, and God helped us all to want to "open up" our hearts to His larger vision and plan. Some rethinking and vision were needed, but our three commitments aided us in crossing from old, familiar territories out into new frontiers of prayer experiences. Our group now has a strong inner core of fifteen to eighteen people who act as a balance wheel to the constant flow of guests. God is helping us maintain patterns of intimacy, but also to be more expansive and broad. Many seeds are planted, many people catch a view of what the Body of Christ can be and many answers to prayer come through believing prayer. It's exciting!

Do you see tall cottonwoods on the horizon? Are you living near a watering hole? Are you a part of the corporate Body of Christ in intercession? If you are not, you are missing one of the main avenues of growth in prayer.

A New Kind of Prayer Meeting

Jack W. Hayford

Senior pastor, The Church On
The Way; author; from Van
Nuys, California

For most people the words *prayer meeting* conjure images of a
small, musty group of irrelevant people who gather out of su-
perstition, mumble heavenward and then dissolve quietly into
the night. Not so with our Wednesday night gatherings. The
people who come have a mission; they are more like an army
on the march.

The key is intercession.

At one of our first meetings someone suggested we pray
about an earthquake in Central America.

"That disaster deserves prayer," I answered. "How shall we
pray about it?"

At first, everyone looked uncomfortable. Weren't such matters simply "put into the hands of the Lord"? I confess this had
been my reaction, too, for the early part of my ministry, that we
turn these problems over to the Lord and He was responsible
for whatever happened.

"Let's ask the Holy Spirit to show us how we should pray
about national disasters," I suggested.

We did so and over the next half hour we arrived at these requests:

1. Pray for the bereaved, that the Spirit of God would comfort them.
2. Pray against bitterness's finding an entrenched place in hearts that would blame God for the earthquake.
3. Pray for Gospel workers and believers to demonstrate the love, power and life of Jesus unto the salvation of souls.
4. Pray for rescue workers and relief agencies, that their efforts would be enabled by God's blessing and international help.
5. Pray that our interest would not wane following this prayer time, but that we would continue to pray, and that God would show us how to help in addition to praying.

Can you imagine what happened? The people prayed fervently, with faith and conviction. We sought God earnestly to take a hand in the situation and demonstrate His power. Later we watched the papers and other media for evidence of answers. At the same time, we decided to receive an offering to send to an appropriate relief agency; and, as it turned out, our own denomination became engrossed immediately in such relief through our work there.

Two or three years later, our missionary from that nation visited our congregation and told us what happened following the earthquake, knowing of our interest through the gift we had sent. All were thrilled to hear him recite specific matters of record that revealed God's hand moving along the exact lines we had prayed about!

That request established our basic stance. A new mood began to govern our praying. We no longer "just prayed." Instead we *defined* our objectives in prayer, *believed* our God would answer and *served* the situation in any way we could when that was possible.

The result of this was that we became excited about intercession. All our prayers became more specific. In the process, one Scripture passage became especially important to us:

> I exhort therefore, that, first of all, supplications, prayers, intercessions, and giving of thanks, be made for all men; for kings, and for all that are in authority; that we may lead a quiet and peaceable life in all godliness and honesty.
>
> 1 Timothy 2:1–2, KJV

Not until that moment had I seen it: Such praying is a priority for the entire Body of believers! Explicitly, people will enjoy "a quiet and peaceable life" only in a nation where people are praying.

With that, we began a pilgrimage to learn the meaning of intercession—a pilgrimage that continues to this day. Soon after that evening, for several months, we set 7:14 P.M. each Wednesday as a reminder of our national intercessory assignment on the basis of this passage:

> If my people, which are called by my name, shall humble themselves, and pray, and seek my face, and turn from their wicked ways; then will I hear from heaven, and will forgive their sin, and will heal their land.
>
> 2 Chronicles 7:14, KJV

One teacher has defined intercession as "Holy Spirit-directed and Holy Spirit-empowered prayer." That is what we learned— to seek and allow the Holy Spirit to show us what to pray for and how to go about it. Just as we had learned more about prayer as a result of that one request concerning the earthquake, so now we are learning new dimensions of prayer every week concerning our nation's needs.

Then, one night, the wife of one of our elders spoke this prophecy:

"My people, I have called you before to pray for your land, but this day I call you to a broader field of responsibility . . . to make this place a house of prayer for all nations."

How could we pray for every nation? The sheer magnitude of it boggled my mind! But by waiting on God, we found a path for this added ministry, and today virtually every nation on earth is sustained before God's throne in prayer by our congregation.

Separate groups in our church now carry an international prayer assignment; and I have asked every member of the congregation to ask the Holy Spirit what nation He would have him or her pray for.

Today, at family prayer times, each person may mention "his" or "her" nation. Some of our people initiate programs of contact with "their" nation. Some have visited the land for which they pray, and others carry on correspondence with missionaries serving there.

In addition, we believe God has assigned us other prayer responsibilities. The needs of individuals are written on cards and circulated to prayer groups, sometimes read aloud at a service. We want people who face cancer to have a special place of prayer-refuge among us. We believe deeply that yet another youth revival awaits this nation, intended by God to exceed the Jesus Movement of the late '60s and early '70s.

The Holy Spirit of intercession is a Spirit of travail; and where we travail in prayer, life comes forth and the Kingdom of God extends its triumph over the works of darkness.

VIII
Going Deeper

When you begin to intercede seriously for others and discover that a specific prayer has been answered, there is a first-blush surge of excitement. "Why this thing really works! Where have I been?" With new enthusiasm you decide to get deeply involved.

It is then that you discover the depths of intercession. Like the peeling of an onion, there is layer after layer of riches to uncover.

The Cost of Intercession

Colleen Townsend Evans

Author of *The Vine Life, Make
Me Like You, Lord* and other
books; from Washington, D.C.

God blesses intercessors in very special ways—perhaps because He knows only too well the cost to us of being one of His
prayer warriors.

First, *the cost of time*. To be an intercessor means we must find
time to be absolutely alone with God. To love people and to be
an intercessor takes time.

I used to plan my life so full that there really was not enough
time to do those things I wanted to do for others. Then I came
to the place where I took my datebook and began to margin out
time for people. Time for prayer. And enough quiet hours to do
this. That means saying no to certain requests. It means I had
to allow God to prune my life so that I had time to do these
things on behalf of others that God was calling me to do.

Second, there is for the intercessor *the price of aloneness*. Jesus,
on that last night when death was rattling right at His door,
asked several of His closest friends to go away with Him to
pray. But they were not prepared for late night, lonely hours,
and fell asleep on Him.

As an intercessor, be prepared to spend some very quiet

alone hours. Not *lonely* because you will be with the Lord, but alone in the sense that you cannot expect other people always to share the things that you have received as your concern to pray over.

The third cost of intercession to you is *energy*. Intercession is work; it is hard work. It takes time and concentration. If someone asks me to pray and I do not write down the names of the people they want me to pray for and the name of the person who made the request, I am likely to forget it.

It is not unspiritual to have a list—to write things out, to be specific. I know that I am just not able to remember things well enough on my own, but if I write them down and am reminded because I have those names right there, then the Holy Spirit can pray through me for those people.

I also use that list to cross things off when the prayers are answered. That is a wonderful affirmation and encouragement in itself. As intercessors we often will pray for people we will never see face to face. We will pray for people and never know whether our prayers have been answered. This is a selfless prayer—when we pray without seeing the results—when we pray knowing and trusting that God is at work. Are we offended when we invest our energy and time in something and then do not see or know or have the joy of understanding what God has done?

As intercessors we will be put in quiet corners where no one will know what we are doing and God will seal our lips so that we are not to boast or talk about what we are doing. At those times I think Jesus says to us, "Blessed are you when you are not offended in Me."

Then, fourth, there is *the cost of obedience*. And obedience will very often lead to involvement: in other people's lives—and occasionally in causes or activities.

Years ago we moved to an affluent community in California. When we arrived there, I discovered that there were no people of other races allowed in that community. I began to pray about that. As a result of my prayers I was asked to join an open housing committee.

That simple prayer of "God, do something about our community," got me into a lot of trouble! If you begin to pray about your community and you begin to ask God to change it, He may lead you to situations and to causes and to issues in which He will ask you not just to pray, but He will ask you to get up off your knees and go out and do something about the very things you are praying for. So prayer can lead to involvement and when we are obedient to God, there will often be a cost.

On another occasion, I began praying for a well-known woman neighbor whom I sensed had a problem with alcohol. One afternoon the phone rang and it was this friend. The longer we talked, the stranger her voice became. Finally, silence. I thought I heard her phone drop to the floor.

Frightened, I drove to her house and knocked on her door. No answer. Finally, I climbed the fence at the back of her house and walked to the patio from where I could see her stretched out in the family room of their home, behind the sliding glass doors.

Inside, I knelt down beside her and could get no pulse. Then I called the police. The rescue squad arrived and resuscitated her.

Later, this woman faced up to her problem and asked the Lord of lords and King of kings to come into her life. He did for her what she could *never* have done for herself. She now is being used in a powerful way to reach out to others in the name of Christ.

The point is—prayer will sometimes get us involved in risky things; obedience can lead into involvement.

The fifth cost of intercession is *persecution.* Prayer is warfare and when we are fighting evil, we simply have to know that evil is going to fight back. Jesus warned us that this would be so. When we stand with and for Christ, we are being identified with Him.

Peter wrote, "Don't be amazed when suffering comes your way, . . . rather, praise God that you bear His name."

I have come to the place in my life in which I have had to stop asking such questions as, "Why do I have to suffer? Why do people I love have to suffer? Why do good people have to suffer?" Instead, I say, "Lord, You told us that the more we are growing in Your likeness, the more the world will hate us and the more suffering and persecution will come our way. So rather than ask why, Lord, I ask that You make me willing to bear whatever it is I must bear in order to be more like You, in order to bear Your name in this world."

Suffering is simply part of the cost of being an intercessor and part of the cost of discipleship. We can draw strength from these words: He who is within us is greater than he who is in the world (see 1 John 4:4). Jesus who lives within us is far more powerful than Satan who roars around the world. And with Christ within us, we can take whatever cost, whatever suffering, whatever persecution comes our way.

Persistence in Prayer

George R. Callahan

Pastor, New Covenant Church;
from Pompano Beach, Florida

Some people will have you believe that God is like a celestial Santa Claus. Just ask Him for what you want and He will give it to you. Period. And you need not ask but once, for if you ask Him more than once it is a sign you lack faith.

Those who have majored in prayer and intercession know how false this teaching is. Sooner or later comes the dark night of the soul when life seems futile, God feels far away and no one appears to be listening to your prayers. In fact, more times than not, what you ask for is not given you. But do not quit. If the prayer is not plain selfish or silly, keep praying.

The story in Mark of the four men who brought the paralyzed man to Jesus is a striking example of persistence. These four must have been faithful, determined friends who had been praying for the sick man for some time. When they arrived at the house where Jesus was staying, the place was so mobbed with people, there was no way to get inside.

They did not quit and go home. Instead, they studied the situation, then removed part of the roof and let the man down through the opening on his pallet into the presence of Jesus.

How Jesus must have loved their tenacity! "Rise, take up your pallet and go home," He commanded. And the paralyzed man was instantly healed and did as Jesus commanded.

I think there are four reasons why God wants us to be persistent with prayer.

First, we will never learn real dependence on God if the answers come quick and easy. I think God is saying, "Don't put Me in a box; don't paste a label on Me; don't try to coerce Me. My ways are not your ways."

If I as a parent give in to my child's every wish, what a little monster I will create—and what a crippled adult this child will become! And how this child-adult will hate me in later life for giving in to his or her every whim. Like a good father, God knows what is best for us.

When God says no to our prayer request, a loving firmness often comes through. "Not today," He may be saying, or "Try Me later," or "Re-think your wish." He never wants us to stop praying. He wants us to keep asking and rethinking our needs, all the time learning more about Him through the Word.

Remember—God is not going to bend. He is going to have His way with us sooner or later.

Second, God wants us to persist in prayer because this will assure Him we have examined our motives.

Let's be honest, how pure are our motives? Re-examine prayers that are not answered. Is there an underlying selfishness throughout them? Do we bargain with God?

As we persist in prayer, the truth will come out and sometimes we will see clearly why the request was not granted.

One new husband began praying that his wife would be more loving to him. He had been asking this for weeks when the light came. He needed to change his prayer and ask that he learn how to be more loving to his wife! That prayer was answered at once, probably because it was selfless and the result of new, mature thinking. And his wife responded accordingly!

So if your prayer is not answered at once, keep praying as you examine the motives behind it.

Third, God wants us to come to believe that He truly knows what is best for us.

The issue here is trust. Have we learned to trust God? A woman told me recently, "I have great faith because God always answers my prayers."

I replied as gently as I knew how, "I don't think that has anything to do with faith. To me, faith is believing when I can't see an answer—'the substance of things hoped for, the evidence of things not seen.' "

Actually, hers was not faith but presumption. Faith is when I dial God and the phone rings and rings and no one answers. Yet I know He is there. Faith is not having it when you want it, but still believing in the One who does not give it to you.

Faith is knowing that God has your alcoholic husband in the palm of His hand though there is no evidence of that. Faith is knowing that God has your rebellious children in the palm of His hand, though there is no evidence of that either.

The greatest leap of faith I ever made was in crisis time when I did not believe I had anybody to stand with me, not even my wife. God had me stripped of any support system around me. He can do that—isolate you in the midst of the whole world—and the only Person left is God. But at that point, I made what was probably the most important decision of my life. I decided that God was enough. And my life was blessed.

When we pray for something we desperately want—and do not get it—can we say, "Though You reject my request, yet I trust you"?

Fourth, I believe there are times when God does not answer our prayers because He is not sure we will give Him the glory.

That makes God seem selfish, you say. Not so. He wants the glory given to Him, not because He needs it but because we need to give it to Him. If we do not, we will end up glorifying ourselves. It can happen like this:

You pray for help with your business. An idea comes that works. Money and success follow. It is so easy to forget you sought God's help; easier still to take credit for the new idea. Self-glorification follows.

The ideal stance is to keep praying for answers. If nothing happens, keep praying. God may be at work in ways you will never know. If an answer comes, give God the glory and go on to the next thing.

Christ's teaching includes this verse: "And I tell you, ask and it shall be given you; seek and you will find; knock, and it will be opened to you." Some may view that verse as Christ's rather pat promise to answer our every prayer. Not if you read the verse in light of what Jesus said to His disciples just before. He told them that if they went to a friend's house at midnight to borrow three loaves of bread, the friend would probably refuse them due to the lateness of the hour. "But I'll tell you this," continued Jesus. "If you keep knocking long enough, he will get up and give you what you want—just because of your persistence" (Luke 11:5–8, LB).

Then Jesus gave His clarion call to persistent prayer: *Ask, seek, knock.* Eventually the prayer may be discarded because it is too selfish or revised to fit God's purposes or continued as is to meet God's timing.

Jesus summed it up, "For everyone who asks, receives. And he who seeks, finds. And to him who knocks, it will be opened."

Prophetic Intercession

Nancy Oliver LeSourd

Attorney and law firm partner;
from Herndon, Virginia

My friend Judy Ross is a nurse who started her own business recently. She is also a prayer partner in a rather unusual way. You see, Judy has the gift of prophetic intercession. On March 13, 1985, her special prayer gift probably saved my life.

At 3:00 P.M. that day, a Wednesday, Judy had been deep in thought over a business problem when the Lord tapped her for duty. *Pray for Nancy* was the thought He placed on her mind. Obedient to the call, Judy slipped away to a quiet place, got down on her knees and prayed fervently for me for almost an hour. At 4:00 she had release from the Lord to stop praying. Concerned, she telephoned me at the office. She was informed that the hospital had just called and I had been in an accident.

Early that Wednesday afternoon the culmination of several weeks of research and preparation was in a file on my desk ready to be dropped in my briefcase. I was about to head to Washington National Airport to fly to Tulsa where I would speak to a group of educators on legal issues in private education. An exciting opportunity! I had taught high school students for five years before entering law school. Now a full-fledged lawyer with a Washington firm, I was in a position to help private school administrators handle some of their legal matters.

At 3:00 P.M. I tossed my briefcase onto the backseat of my little Honda Civic and headed for the airport. I tuned the radio to a Christian station. There was a cheerful praise song playing and I sang along heartily. I thanked God for His help in my preparing to speak at the conference.

My thoughts wandered. I was single, almost 32 years old. Did God have the right man for me? If so, when and how would I meet him? Or did He want me in some kind of singles ministry? Whatever—I wanted His plan for my life.

I was still several miles from the airport when out of the corner of my eye I saw a car barrel through a stop sign. "Lord," I cried out, "he's going to hit me!"

The approaching car crashed into me broadside causing my little car to roll first to the left, hit the median and then flip end over end several times until it came to rest upside down two lanes away. The only sounds I heard were the crunch of metal and the splintering of glass.

I was still conscious. I had landed on my neck and right shoulder. I could feel the shards of glass pressing into my scalp as my head rested on the shattered window and glass-strewn pavement. All I saw was a sea of legs and upside-down faces. The drama of the event had gathered quite a crowd all leaning over to peer at this woman dangling in the car. The radio was still playing praise music.

The rescue squad arrived, pondering the dilemma of how to extract me from the car without moving my neck. It took them twenty minutes to cut through the metal of the car. I had left my office at 3:00. The accident had occurred at 3:15 and I arrived at the hospital at 3:45. Although there was muscle damage, amazingly no broken bones or stitches needed.

When Judy came to visit me in the hospital, we compared notes. A bit awestruck, Judy realized the specific role she had been given by the Lord—to intercede for my protection.

That call to pray for my protection was *prophetic intercession*, a ministry distinct from other types of prayer. It begins with the heart of God, is then channeled through the heart of the one praying and results in the plan of God being accomplished in the life of another. God sees what is coming and seeks a prophet to whom He can give the message, "This is coming: Warn." Or, "This is coming: Pray." Through the obedience of the prophet to answer that call, God intercedes in circumstances to protect and guard that which is His.

Biblical prophets were those who shared God's thoughts with God's people. Often these thoughts took the form of warnings or exhortations. Prophets encouraged others to abandon sin, abstain from certain acts or repent. Prophets warned of impending judgment. At other times, prophets acted to protect.

When God calls us to prophetic intercession, He may give us a warning to give to another or burden us to pray for the protection of another, even when that person is unaware of any danger. God may prevent a thing from happening or He may protect in the midst of the tragedy, as He did with me.

God used His prophet Elisha several times this way to protect Israel against the Syrians (2 Kings 6:8–23).

When Paul was a prisoner, he engaged in prophetic intercession when he alerted the centurion aboard a ship bound for Italy that the voyage would be extremely dangerous (Acts 27:9–44).

What happens if God should tap one of us for the duty of prophetic intercession? First, we must recognize the call. The call may come through a direct vision of what is to happen. At other times, like Judy, we may get a sense or premonition of danger surrounding a certain person or group of people.

Second, we should obey the call when it interrupts our plan or activities. If the Lord calls us to pray, there may be an urgent need for someone's protection at that very moment. Even when you cannot get away, as in a business meeting, a quick prayer of protection can be offered.

Third, we should answer the call to pray without making assumptions about what God should do. Sometimes the Lord will prevent a thing from happening. Sometimes He will let it happen but protect those in the midst of it. The call is to pray.

The responsibility for the outcome is God's alone. He knows the condition of men's hearts and the plan He has for their lives.

My accident was not averted, but God used it for good. During my six-month period of recuperation, God had some things to accomplish in my life to prepare me to meet the man I was to marry. Without that slowed-down period to search the Scriptures and examine my heart, I might not have recognized this particular man, Jeffrey LeSourd, as God's choice for me, or been ready to accept the call to be his wife.

Earning that "Gained Position"

Norman Grubb

Author of *Rees Howells Intercessor*; from Ft. Washington, Pennsylvania

Believers in general have regarded intercession as just some form of rather intensified prayer. This is true. And there are three qualities that develop in an intercessor, which are not necessarily found in the ordinary prayer: 1) identification, 2) agony, 3) authority.

The *identification* of the intercessor with the ones for whom he intercedes is seen perfectly in the Savior. Of Jesus it was said that *He poured out His soul unto death: and He bare the sin of many, and made intercession for the transgressors.*

As the divine Intercessor, interceding for a lost world, Jesus drained the cup of our lost condition to its last drop. He "tasted death for every man." To do that, in the fullest possible sense, He sat where we sit. By taking our nature upon Himself, by being tempted in all points like as we are, by becoming poor for our sakes and finally by being made sin for us, He gained the position in which, through effective pleadings with the Father, "He is able to save to the uttermost them that come unto God by Him."

Identification is thus the first law of the intercessor. He

pleads effectively because, in a sense, he gives his life for those for whom he pleads; he is their genuine representative; he has submerged his self-interest in their needs and sufferings, and as far as possible has literally taken their place.

Secondly, it is through the Holy Spirit that we see the *agony* of this ministry. It is the Holy Spirit who "maketh intercession for us with groanings which cannot be uttered." This Intercessor, now with us on earth, has no hearts upon which He can lay His burdens, and no bodies through which He can suffer and work, except the hearts and bodies of those who are His dwelling place. Through them He does His intercessory work on earth, and they become intercessors by reason of the Intercessor being within them. It is real life to which He calls them, the very same kind of life, in lesser measure, that the Savior Himself lived on earth.

Before the Holy Spirit can lead one into such a life of intercession, He first has to deal with that person's love of money, personal ambition, appetites of the body and the love of life itself. *All that makes a believer live for his own comfort or advantage, for his own advancement, even for his own circle of friends, has to go to the cross.* This is no theoretical death but a real crucifixion with Christ, such as only the Holy Ghost Himself can make actual in the experience of His servant. Thus, Paul's testimony becomes ours: "I have been and still am crucified with Christ." The self is released from itself to become the agent of the Holy Ghost.

As crucifixion proceeds, intercession begins. By calls to outward obedience, the Spirit begins to live His own life of love and sacrifice for a lost world through His cleansed vessel. We see this in Moses, the young intercessor, leaving the palace by free choice to identify himself with his slave-brethren. Later we see him reach the very same summit of intercession, when the wrath of God was upon the Israelites for their idolatry and their destruction was imminent. It is not his body he now offers for them as intercessor, but his immortal soul: "If Thou wilt forgive their sin—; and if not, blot me, I pray Thee, out of The Book."

The apostle Paul offered his body, through the Holy Ghost,

as a living sacrifice, that the Gentiles might have the Gospel. This is the intercessor in action. When the Holy Ghost really. lives His life in a chosen vessel, there is no limit to the extremes to which He will take him, in His passion to warn and save the lost.

Every greatly used instrument of God has been, in his measure, an intercessor: Wesley for backsliding England; Booth for the down-and-outs; Hudson Taylor for China.

If the intercessor knows *identification* and *agony*, he also knows *authority*. He so identifies with the sufferer that it gives him a prevailing place with God. A position of authority. He moves God. He even causes God to change His mind.

Moses, by intercession, became the savior of the Israelites and prevented their destruction. Paul's supreme act of intercession for God's chosen people resulted in the great revelation given him at that time of worldwide evangelization and the final salvation of Israel (Romans 10 and 11).

This authority is often spoken of as "the gained position of intercession." The obedience to prayer is fulfilled, the inner wrestlings and groanings take their full course, and then "the word of the Lord comes." The weak praying vessel is clothed with authority by the Holy Ghost and can speak the word of deliverance. "Greater works" are done. Not only this, but a new position in grace is gained and maintained.

When an intercessor has gained that place of intercession (or authority) in a certain realm, then he has entered into "the grace of faith." At that point the measureless sea of God's grace is open to him.

The Mercy Prayer

Catherine Marshall

Founder of Breakthrough; author of fifteen books including *A Man Called Peter* and *Christy*

No matter how much you think you have learned about a subject, there is always more. It was my Florida friend Betty who told me about the *mercy prayer* at a time of need in my life.

She had been attending a baptism in the Episcopal Church. The baby being christened was not only crying but even screaming at times. "I could see how embarrassed the infant's parents were and I felt such compassion for them," Betty said. "But then the thought dropped into my mind that there was no way I could possibly be feeling more compassionate than Jesus.

"So I simply prayed, 'Lord Jesus, have mercy on that baby and his father and mother.'

"Catherine, it was remarkable. The crying stopped immediately as if a faucet had been turned off."

Betty went on to explain that she had first "discovered" the mercy prayer eight years before when her husband had undergone a serious cancer operation. His recovery had then seemed threatened last summer when his doctor suspected a return of cancer.

"It was a time of great agony," Betty told me. "All my

praying—hours of it—finally jelled down into a single heartfelt plea, 'Father in heaven, will You have mercy on us simply for Jesus' sake?' "

The result? The finest cancer specialists at Duke pronounced it a false alarm. There was no return of the cancer.

Since talking with Betty I have spent several of my morning prayer times asking the Lord for insights about the validity and effectiveness of the Mercy Prayer. Passage after passage of Scripture was brought to my attention. I saw that many of Jesus' healings, as recorded in the Gospels, came as the result of a prayer for mercy by some sufferer.

There were, for instance, the two blind men sitting by the side of the road one day as Jesus was leaving Jericho (Matthew 20:29–34). Hearing that this was Jesus passing by, the two men cried out, "Have mercy on us, O Lord, thou son of David."

The crowd following the Master rebuked the men, telling them to keep quiet. But the blind men were desperate, so they only cried the louder, "Have mercy on us, O Lord."

And Jesus, standing still and giving the men His full attention, asked what they wanted of Him. When they begged Jesus to open their eyes, *He had compassion on them*, touched the eyes of both men and immediately each received his sight.

Then there was the time Jesus encountered ten lepers (Luke 17:11–14). Since lepers were ostracized from public gatherings, these ten men stood at a distance crying almost in unison, "Jesus, Master, have mercy on us."

The Master did not question each man about how well he had kept the Law or how righteous he was. Out of Jesus' overflowing compassionate love, He healed all ten on the spot.

"Go at once, and show yourselves to the priests for proof of your healing," He told them. "Your faith has *already* made you clean."

Faith in what or in whom? The connecting link is our belief that God loves each of us far more than does the most warmhearted person we know; that He heals simply because He wants us to have the joy of abundant health.

"I will have mercy, and not sacrifice: for I am not come to call the righteous, but sinners to repentance," Jesus said (Matthew 9:13, KJV).

The apostle Paul's statements give us the same truth: "Blessed be the God and Father of our Lord Jesus Christ, the Father of mercies and God of all comfort, who comforts us in all our affliction . . ." (2 Corinthians 1:3–4, RSV).

"So then [God's gift] is not a question of human will and human effort, but of God's mercy . . ." (Romans 9:16, TAB).

In other words, you and I are dependent—whether we recognize this or not—on His love and mercy.

An Inner Voice also instructed me to look in the Episcopal *Book of Common Prayer* for that prayer always included as a part of the sacrament of Holy Communion:

> Lord, have mercy upon us.
> Christ, have mercy upon us.
> Lord, have mercy upon us.

When I searched the word *mercy* in Cruden's *Concordance*, I found a surprisingly long list of Scripture references. Moreover, Alexander Cruden's original words of description set down in 1769 are rich food for thought:

> Mercy signifies that the essential perfection is in God, whereby He pities and relieves the miseries of His creatures.

and

> "Grace" flows from "mercy" as its fountain.

The insights about the Mercy Prayer were not over yet. During a wakeful time in the middle of the next night, the Inner Voice (there is no mistaking it!) forcibly reminded me of the particular words of the promise God had given me on the morning of Peter Marshall's death back in 1949. It had come as I had been about to leave the hospital room in which my husband's body lay. Even as I had reached for the doorknob, it was as if a giant hand had stopped me. Then clearly and emphatically, yet with tenderness combined with surprising power, had come, *Goodness and mercy shall follow you all the days of your life.*

And now so many years later, deep in the night, the same Voice was saying, *Note that word* mercy, *Catherine.* My *goodness,* My *mercy. That's what is following you and will surround you to the end of your earthly walk. Lean back on that. Depend on it.*

How needed that assurance was for me at that particular moment in time years ago! How needed today in our troubled age!

For the resounding validity of the Mercy Prayer all through Scripture is meant for everyone: "The Lord is good; his *mercy* is everlasting; and his truth endureth to all generations" (Psalm 100:5, KJV).

Why Intercessors Fast

Leonard LeSourd

Chairman of Breakthrough; former editor, *Guideposts* magazine; associate publisher, Chosen Books; from Lincoln, Virginia

Let's face it, abstaining from food as a spiritual discipline is not very popular among Christians today. It can produce discomfort, sometimes ridicule. Among certain non-Christians the fast has been used—and also scorned—as a political ploy. Jesus rebuked certain religious people of His time when they fasted to impress others.

Not until I was 55 years old did I ever seriously consider fasting. Then, in 1974, I was faced with a decision to resign from a well-paying position I had enjoyed for 28 years in order to go into a book publishing partnership. There were huge risks in such a change. Just to pray for guidance about it did not seem enough. To hear God's word, I felt I was supposed to shift gears into a higher level of spiritual consciousness.

I was led to consider three kinds of fast: (1) *The absolute fast* where one does without both food and water; (2) *the normal fast* where one does without food but drinks water; and (3) *the partial fast*, a sharp restriction of diet. I chose the last and for two days partook of nothing but liquids and an occasional cracker. At the beginning of the fast, I placed myself in a prayer framework where I maintained a continuing dialogue with God as I went through normal activities.

Several things happened. I never got hungry. I had more instead of less vitality. My thinking was more sharply focused. I felt closer to the Lord than ever before. And I had the distinct guidance that God was saying yes to the change in career.

So I did make the change and have been blessed by it in every way.

Did the fasting prayer become a regular part of my life from then on? No, it didn't. I learned that fasting is not something I decide to do, but is to be initiated by the Lord.

Several years later when a group of us started The New Covenant Church in Pompano Beach, Florida, a piece of property became available on which we could build our church home. To acquire it, a large (for us) down payment was needed. It seemed 'way beyond our reach. The guidance came we were to pray and fast. We did for one day a week for a period of several months.

Again there was a shift of gears into a higher spiritual level. The food discipline seemed to reduce self-centeredness, increase focus on the higher objective and thus increase the prayer power. The seemingly impossible goal was reached only hours before the deadline.

My conviction about fasting is that it is important—much more important than we as Christians have been willing to admit. *Especially important for intercessors.* Though not a panacea for every ill, fasting may provide us a key to unlock doors that other keys have failed. It can be a window opening up new horizons into the unseen world.

Jesus made several points to His disciples about fasting: He said to them, "When you fast . . . ," meaning there was no question about their need to do it. He also warned them (Matthew 6:16) not to pray or fast in such a way as to receive praise from men.

When Christians ask the question, "What can I gain from fasting?" they miss the point. Fasting is done unto God (Zechariah 7:5). In Isaiah 58, God reminds His people that fasting, like prayer, should begin with God. Through the Holy

Spirit He places a burden upon us to pray and fast and we respond to that burden.

That God initiates the fast does not relieve us of the responsibility to recognize the rightness and need for it. We should be ready and willing to exercise the self-discipline involved. When Joel cried, "Sanctify a fast," he meant *set it apart for God.* When we do this, we will be caught up in wonder, love and praise as we fast unto God.

It seems clear that the intercessor has another tool in his prayer arsenal when he or she is willing to fast. Andrew Murray put it this way: "Fasting helps to express, to deepen and to confirm the resolution that we are ready to sacrifice anything to attain that which we seek in the Kingdom of God."

To sum it up, here are guidelines for the intercessor:

1. Seek the Lord's direction if and when you are to use the fasting prayer in connection with any of those people or situations for which you are praying.
2. Know your body well enough to choose the right kind of fast (absolute, normal or partial).
3. Begin modestly (a single meal, a full day, three straight days).
4. Do it with as much secrecy as possible.
5. Leave the results to God.

Remember, fasting is designed to make prayer mount up as on eagles' wings. It is intended to usher the suppliant into the audience chamber of the King and to drive back the oppressing powers of darkness, thereby loosening their hold on those being prayed for. Fasting will definitely give an edge to man's intercessions and power to his petition.

Travailing Prayer

June G. Coxhead

Radio talk show host; from
Christchurch, New Zealand

It had been one of those days. Running late, I raced down the basement steps to the room where our regular Wednesday night intercessors' group met and took the one vacant metal chair in the circle.

There were about twenty people present. Across from me a stylishly dressed woman in her cream silk suit was sharing a deep concern.

"What is it?" I whispered to my next-door neighbor.

"It's Pat," she whispered back. "Her cancer is in its last stages. The doctors don't expect her to last the night out. But it's not Pat we're troubled about. She's prepared. It's her husband, Charles."

I didn't know Charles, but from the group discussion I surmised he was a bitter man who didn't share his wife's faith, was angry at God and emotionally unable to cope with Pat's impending death. I could identify with his hurt in my head. In my heart I felt nothing. My mind was whirring over another project I had been tackling that day.

The group had been praying for some minutes when, as

frequently happened in this midweek meeting, several dropped to their knees and started weeping. Crouched on the thin, green felt basement carpet, head in hands, their gentle sobbing soon developed into deep sighs of anguish.

Normally I would have been there with them. Tonight as I sat back unattached, I found myself questioning. Was what I was witnessing really an expression of God's Holy Spirit or was it merely a fleshy display of human emotion?

I looked around the group. We were not a bunch of novices. There were a few faces I didn't recognize, but the core had been meeting together for many years. The pastor's wife was there, as was the leader of our children's ministry. Her husband, a local politician, sat next to her. Our fair-haired leader looked young for his 35 years, but he had spent ten of those on the mission field. I myself had been in a full-time Christian service for thirteen.

The meeting functioned under the close supervision of our pastor and only those with a genuine heart for intercession were encouraged to attend. There was no room for the casual onlooker. Yet this is what I was being, someone attempting to judge a spiritual activity with human eyes. A useless exercise. I recalled Paul's warning in 1 Corinthians 2:14, that the unspiritual person is unable to understand the gifts of the Spirit. They are spiritually discerned.

I could judge the genuineness of what was happening only if I were in the Spirit myself. I wasn't. For all I was contributing I may as well have been a thousand miles away. My reasoning? It had been a hectic day. I was tired. I did not know Charles. I would sit this prayer-round out and let those who knew him wage war on his behalf.

I shuffled uncomfortably on my metal chair as a verse flashed into my mind. "Bear ye one another's burdens." Conviction hit. I might not know Charles, but neither did the Good Samaritan know the wounded roadside traveler when he ministered to him.

Not knowing him was not an excuse. My sin was I had not made myself available to the Holy Spirit. I edged my way to where the crouched figures were sobbing, placed my hand softly on a shoulder and began to intercede with them for this hurting man.

What did Charles look like? Was he thin, fat, tall or short? I had no idea. But as I knelt there, God gave me insight into his heart and through the Spirit I was able to identify with his grief and pain.

Soon deep sobs were rising from within me. It was nothing I had worked up. If I had wanted, I could have stopped it at any time. But I chose to let the cries of anguish flow. By the time I rose from my knees some two hours later, a heart transformation had taken place. I carried a concern for a man I had never met.

How could this happen? How could I be so distant one minute and experience such concern the next? It happened because I had touched God's heart. I had experienced what Paul describes in Romans 8:26 as the sighs or groanings of the Spirit that are too deep for words.

This "travail" of intercession, as many term it, is in essence another gift of God's Spirit and, as with any gift, it grows and develops as we continue to avail ourselves of it. But in exercising it, we need to take care.

Travail is not a gift to be taken lightly or used carelessly. It can be counterfeited and abused and should therefore be exercised in submission to recognized leadership and used only with extreme caution in a public meeting. It is good to remember that anyone truly being inspired by God's Spirit will never be out of control. Just as the spirit of the prophet is subject to the prophet, so with travail.

In our group's experience, we have discovered that travail has many dimensions: heart identification with both God and man; the tussle of spiritual warfare; and the struggle of bringing to birth. It is an exciting, exhilarating dimension of prayer through which, as I experienced that night with Charles, we can know the thrill of concern for someone we have never met.

IX
In Search of a Miracle

The phone rings. You lift the receiver and hear the words, "Pray for Jane. She has inoperable cancer."

A difficult assignment. How do you pray for a miracle?

Prayer warriors deal with such requests daily. They have no power to work miracles, but they know how to contact the One who does.

The Soaking Prayer

Francis MacNutt

Author; director of Christian Healing Ministries; from Jacksonville, Florida

I made a discovery some years ago while praying for arthritis patients. Several whose hands were crippled with this disease were healed dramatically; this usually happened at large prayer meetings. But, for the most part, when I prayed individually for such people, a little improvement would take place: The fingers would straighten a little, the wrist and fingers would be able to bend a little more; often the pain would be reduced and disappear. In short, there would be a noticeable change, but nothing like a complete healing.

So where do you go from there? Certainly, you can thank God for the lessening of the pain, and yet you cannot say the person was cured. Why such a mixed result?

It was pretty clear that more time for prayer was indicated. I soon discovered that if some healing had already started to take place, then further prayer would usually lead to still more healing. As a crude example: If about ten percent of a healing took place through the first prayer, then, after praying for another forty minutes, there might be something like a fifty-percent improvement.

To me this was a new discovery that I had not read anything about. As is usual with a new discovery, it brought a new problem: There was not always that kind of time to give to people. The more I pondered this, the more uncomfortable I felt at seeing people line up for prayer at ten P.M. after an evening service. Seeing the severity of some of their needs, I knew that we could not spend enough time soaking them in prayer.

Another problem: My prayer might make them reluctant to seek out someone else afterward to pray for them at length; they might feel it a lack of faith on their part to add someone else's prayer to mine. I now tell people not to hesitate in seeking someone out to pray at greater length. If they feel improved but not completely healed, then perhaps my prayer will begin their healing and someone else's will finish it.

So I have been teaching people to pray the soaking prayer: for parents to pray for their children; for husbands and wives to pray for each other for all those longtime, deep-down sicknesses that have not responded to briefer prayers. Ailments, such as mental retardation, that are rarely healed in an instant, now seem to be notably improved and occasionally healed by means of parents' soaking the child in prayer over a period of months or years.

Since the soaking prayer takes time, we have developed a very simple way of doing it. First comes a prayer, asking God in the usual way to heal the person. Then, we simply continue to lay our hands on the person in such a way that everyone is comfortable. We can alternate periods of song and silence; we can pray in English or we can pray quietly in tongues.

As I see it, a kind of life or power continues to pour gently into the affected part all during the time we pray. If a team is praying, then it is easy to change places when someone gets tired. There is no reason why we cannot pray for an hour and then take a ten-minute coffee break before coming back to pray again. This continuing prayer can go on as long as we judge is right.

In many ways I find it helps to think of soaking prayer as being like radiation or X-ray therapy. The longer the diseased area is held under the radiation of God's healing power, the more diseased cells are killed. At times you can even see a tumor or growth gradually disappear as you pray.

The problem, of course, with cobalt radiation is that healthy cells get killed, too; the treatment sessions have to be fairly short so that the healthy tissues of the body are not too badly hurt. On the other hand, the wonderful thing about prayer is that there are no harmful side effects. You can pray as long as you want. The only limit imposed is our own strength, since prayer does take something out of us; we have to set limits and rest.

This means that soaking prayer can be something we do at regular intervals; parents can pray for five minutes a day for their retarded child, or we can try praying once a week for fifteen minutes with an arthritic friend. On the other hand, we can decide to spend a whole afternoon or a whole day praying for a friend who has multiple sclerosis.

If we are going to spend considerable time with a person, we should ordinarily have some indication—through a gift of knowledge or some other sign—that we should spend that much time. Furthermore, if we pray too long with a person and nothing much happens, he naturally tends to feel guilty—as if he had failed to meet expectations. So, ordinarily, I only pray for a longer time when something really begins to happen soon after the prayer has begun.

I once prayed for a man in Phoenix who had bone problems in his heel and ankle that made it impossible for him to walk without pain. All the pain left and he was able to run up and down for the first time in years without pain. When I saw him recently he told me the healing had lasted, but it remained at the point to which it had improved at that time; namely, the pain had gone and much mobility had returned. But as we prayed again, still more movement returned to the stiffened ankle. The longer we prayed, the more movement there was; finally, I had to stop because others were waiting, but he and his wife will continue to pray toward a complete healing.

Sometimes what is begun in a short prayer—for example, a

tumor starts to get smaller—may just continue happening for several hours after we have finished praying and the person has gone home. At other times the improvement only seems to go on as long as we keep praying. I do not understand all this; I am just sharing what I have seen, so that you will not limit the way that God works but will remain open to what seems to be called for with each person you pray with.

In June 1975, at the Oregon Camp Farthest Out Conference, we began praying in a group for Bunni Determan, a lovely teenager who was encased in a neck brace because of a severe scoliosis (S-shaped curvature of the spine). Bunni's mother, a nurse, was part of the group and was able to tell after we had prayed for ten minutes that a change had taken place. So we kept praying for two hours and by the end of that time most of the curvature at the top of the spine had been straightened out. The next two days the group, including many of Bunni's teen-age friends, prayed some more—another hour each day—and by the end of the CFO Bunni's back seemed about eighty percent improved. And with continued prayer by her mother and her friends she is now out of her neck brace and is about ninety percent of the way to having a straight back.

Someone always asks why we have to spend so much time praying with people; they point out that Jesus usually healed with a word. We could answer that even Jesus had to pray twice with the one blind man (Mark 8:22–26), and then He encouraged us to persist in asking day and night. For myself I have often found that taking time in prayer is essential; and it works! If anyone can cure a severe chronic illness by a word, I am all for that, but healings probably work gradually through some of us because the life of Jesus in us needs to grow stronger.

Faith as a Little Child

Virginia Lively

Author of *Healing in His Presence*; from Belle Glade, Florida

His eyes are as blue as the sky on a clear day. Interested and inquiring. His hair, cut in a modified Buster Brown, is as shining as sunlight laced with fine gold. He has just turned four years old. His name is Michael. He is my grandson. Last August, Michael, his mother, Linda (my daughter), and I had planned a two-week vacation in the mountains of North Carolina just west of the small town of Waynesville. We had decided to leave Orlando, Florida, on a Friday for the eleven-and-a-half-hour trip by car. I arrived on Thursday to spend the night, which would enable us to get an early start in the morning.

When I pulled into the driveway, Michael came running out of the front door followed by his mother.

"Hi!" I picked him up and kissed him, then greeted Linda. "Mother," she began, "I have so much to do, would you mind terribly if we leave Saturday instead of tomorrow?" "No, of course not," I answered.

During the evening, Michael reminded me repeatedly that we would be roommates. That night, I noticed that he coughed occasionally in his sleep. The next morning the cough was worse.

Sitting on the living room sofa, I watched as he played with his toy animals. He arranged them single file on the edge of the coffee table, then marched them two by two into the ark talking all the while in that special language only understood by one who is a cow or a horse or a tiger. He coughed unceasingly.

"Michael, come here, and let's ask Jesus to heal that cough," I said. Since his mother had prayed with him when he was sick, he was accustomed to prayer for healing.

He left his beloved animals and came to stand at my knee. He closed his eyes tightly and stood very still, waiting. With one arm around his small waist and the other hand on his head I prayed: "Jesus, I know You love Michael and he loves You. I also know it is not Your will for him to be sick. We ask You now to heal this cough and the cause of it so he will be completely well. Thank You. Amen."

Michael echoed, "Amen," resoundingly. He opened his eyes, turned around and went back to his play . . . still coughing.

I continued to pray and he continued to cough during the afternoon. "Michael, how come you're still coughing?" I questioned finally. "I thought we asked Jesus to heal you."

He looked at me thoughtfully, and matter-of-factly replied, "Well, I guess He wasn't home." He sat quietly for a moment and then explained, "He's gone to heal another little boy now, and when He gets through He'll come heal me." (Not sound theology, maybe, but certainly sound faith.) I said simply, "Oh."

We left early the next day for the mountains amid much excitement. Michael napped several times in the car and as the hours passed he seemed to cough less. Linda and I prayed for him while he slept.

When we arrived at our destination we unpacked only the necessary items, ate a light supper and fell into bed early.

Michael was up at first light. "It's time to get up, Mema," he sang cheerily at my bedside. I was aware as we fixed breakfast that the cough had subsided almost entirely.

"Michael, you're not coughing as much as you did yesterday, are you?" I remarked.

"No," he agreed, smiling. "You see, Jesus is healing me . . . one cough at a time," and he danced away to see the mountains from the deck.

He did not try to determine why he had not been healed instantly. He did not wonder if he had enough faith. He did not think he may not be worthy. He did not say he was suffering for Jesus' sake. He did not say it may not be God's will to heal him. He simply *knew* he would be healed, and he was!

Then it occurred to me that he would have had the same kind of faith whether it was for his needs or for others. We adults also had that kind of faith at one time. Some still do. To regain that childlike trust is a happy challenge for us.

What a blessing to be able to answer the Lord's call to persevere in prayer, to knock in faith at His door, to remind Him of His promises and to do so without becoming weary until He grants our petition!

It is to His Son's intercession that the Father responds; in like manner He has called us to intercede for one another. Standing firmly on the promises of God, we refuse to yield, continuing to pray and wait for the answer, even when it is delayed, knowing that the victory is sure.

In Luke 11:5–8, the man finally arose from his bed at midnight and gave bread to his friend because of his persistence. In Luke 18:2–5, the unjust judge granted the widow her request because she was unceasing in her pleading.

Perseverance in prayer is also helpful for us. Delay in the answer should only strengthen our faith, develop steadfastness in us and teach us to trust God implicitly.

Split-Second Prayer

Don V. Bovey

Businessman, grandfather, Bible teacher; from Frederick, Maryland

Every time I get behind the wheel of my car, I place myself in a state of prayer readiness. I learned this lesson several years ago when split-second prayer literally saved my life.

It happened on a Sunday. My wife, Pauline, and I had returned from church to our Frederick, Maryland, home. We ate lunch and I loaded my jeep stationwagon in preparation for a drive to the airport to attend a management seminar in New Jersey.

As I began descending the long, curved driveway in front of our house, I was overcome by the sudden emotion that I should say good-bye again to my wife. How strange! Feeling a bit silly, I stopped the stationwagon in the middle of the driveway, got out and saw Pauline standing by our home, silhouetted against the curved lawn and green woods, looking at our garden.

A thought penetrated my mind. *Don, you may be looking at her for the last time!*

"That's ridiculous!" I replied sternly. "Get ahold of yourself and be off."

I drove toward Washington, turned onto the beltway and

blended in with the traffic. A car to my left suddenly swerved in front of me to reach the exit lane on our right.

The human mind can perform amazing calculations in a split-second. My first thought was for the safety of the lives in the car that was about to hit me.

I stood on my brakes, screaming aloud the short prayer, "No, God!"

The turning auto caught my front bumper and sent my car rolling crazily to the left across two lanes of speeding traffic. Each time my stationwagon rolled over, I moaned, "No, God . . . no, God. . . . " Because of my commitment to Christ, I have never been afraid of death. But I did not want to go out this way.

Miraculously, all of the speeding cars managed to avoid me as my jeep stationwagon smashed against the barrier in the middle of the highway. My car was a mass of twisted metal and shattered glass, resting on its side.

I had been catapulted from the front seat to the rear, flat on my back. I thought to myself, *Open your eyes; see if you are in heaven or Montgomery County, Maryland.*

All about me was the noise of automobiles, shouting people, an enormous traffic snare . . . I was alive in Montgomery County. The first to reach me was a young man who offered me comfort, next a nurse on the way to a nearby hospital, then a physician who looked over my injuries. The Lord delivered a lot of aid in short order.

I was to learn later, through the police report, that a lady traveling directly behind my jeep wagon, witnessed this event. In her deposition, she outlined and confirmed the details. I discovered later, to my astonishment, that this woman had been praying for others just before the accident—for the Pope who had recently been shot and for family needs.

While in this spirit of intercessory prayer she watched my jeep wagon roll across the highway, wondering how anyone could possibly live through such an accident.

"Save that man," was her split-second prayer.

At the same time I was sending forth an intercessory plea—almost a demand—for the Lord to protect those in the passing car in front of me, then I pleaded for Him to intercede on my behalf. Many lives were saved at that moment in time.

How do I explain my inner emotions as I was leaving my home? I do not understand those stabbing thoughts or from where they came, but I do know that prayer can and did change the conditions that could have resulted in my death. I believe that in such emergencies, God sends His angels to intervene in a supernatural way.

Driving in the high-speed lanes of today requires maximum mental and physical alertness. We all need to be fortified with prayer readiness, surrounding ourselves and others all about us constantly.

Wanted! . . . for the Lord

Sandra Simpson LeSourd

Author of *The Compulsive Woman*; from Lincoln, Virginia

I owe my life to a group of people who prayed for me when I was in a seemingly hopeless situation ten years ago. Looking back, there is no other way to account for the inner change that began inside me at that time—a change that led me out of the Montana State Hospital for Mental Disorders into a completely new and productive life.

How I sank into that mess can be covered in a few words: a compulsive behavior pattern that brought on an addiction to alcohol, prescription drugs, nicotine, shopping, certain foods, television. Hopelessness and despair surrounded me.

As one dreary day slid into another, I sat staring through the greasy, nicotine-streaked hospital windows at the dazzling blue sky outside. How had I gotten myself into such a miserable state? I asked myself. Could I ever be well again? So many people had tried to help me: my husband, children, parents, friends. I decided that I was beyond help.

Unbeknownst to me, however, a faithful group of intercessors was praying for me with a burning fervor. Whether they knew me or not, they not only prayed for me, they loved me.

I was a name on their "Ten Most Wanted List," a list they had compiled for desperate cases of people most in need of the Lord.

Every Thursday morning this group of women from First United Methodist Church in Billings, Montana, met to intercede and receive progress reports on people they were praying for. "Lord, please touch Sandy's life. Give her hope. Lift her spirit. Transform her. Send Your emissaries across her path to witness to her, to free her from Satan's bondage."

Later I learned that this group used Scriptures to pray for their "most-wanted" cases. My name would be inserted into the verses like this:

By His stripes, *Sandy* is healed (Isaiah 53:5).

Sandy can do all things through Christ who strengthens her (Philippians 4:13).

For God does not give *Sandy* the spirit of fear, but of power and of love and of a sound mind (2 Timothy 1:7).

For we know that all things work for good for *Sandy* who loves God and has been called according to His purpose (Romans 8:28).

The key to this type of prayer is the power that comes by affirming the best in the person being prayed for. Since I was a mother to three children, this prayer was also used:

Sandy is clothed with strength and dignity. *Sandy* speaks with wisdom and faithful instruction is on her tongue. Her children arise and call her blessed (Proverbs 31).

I would have scoffed in unbelief and heartbreak if I had heard these positive words about me. So far from the truth!

Yet this kind of intercession does work!

Their prayers were beamed into the heavenly kingdom in Jesus' name. They put all their thoughts and imaginations under the blood of Jesus. The devil was rebuked, evil spirits cast out. Some of the women travailed. They asked that holy angels be sent.

In the midst of my despair a beautiful woman named Karen entered the hospital and was assigned to a room adjacent to mine. Her fiancé, it was reported, had been killed in an accident. Karen was inconsolable.

She kept asking for Jesus to help her. Her constant mention of Jesus' name aggravated me so much that I tried to avoid Karen. She kept pursuing me, her chocolate-brown eyes pleading for acceptance.

Late one night I was awakened by someone standing by my bed. It was Karen. She was crying. "Sandy, does Jesus love me?" she asked over and over again.

I had to do something—just had to—so I got up, took Karen in my arms and comforted her as I would a child. "Yes, Karen, Jesus loves you. Jesus *loves* you."

Karen stopped crying and slipped back into her own room. I climbed back into bed. But something was different inside me. I had been touched by—*something!* In reaching out to Karen, a totally *self*-centered person had begun the shift to being *others*-centered.

Last year I called the Montana hospital to see if I could get Karen's address. They remembered me, *but had no record of Karen at all*.

Meanwhile, the Billings women kept praying for me . . . in fact they did for several years.

My next crisis came during a week's visit at home. I had made such good progress since the Karen experience that the hospital staff felt I might make it. The home visits would tell the story.

The first morning at home I awoke terrified. How could I make up to my family for all my irresponsible behavior over the past fifteen years? "Sleep in," came the tempting voice. That was the way I had handled things in the past.

A mighty battle raged inside me. Old ways versus something new. "Get up. *Do it now!*" came a strong new voice.

I got up, showered, put in a load of wash, made a hair appointment and then mopped the kitchen floor.

Major victories . . . aided by a new inner force. A positive inner voice that could be soft and encouraging, but also insistent, strong. I had never had that before. Soon I learned to rebuke the negative, tempting inner voice until it was routed out of my consciousness.

My recovery was underway. A long process—in fact, years—

but step by step I was being freed from the bondages of alcohol, drugs, nicotine, by something I did not understand at all, something supernatural. The power of prayer.

Next came direct contact with these loving, praying women. They invited me to a Bible-study meeting, then persuaded me to attend a healing service one Sunday night in their church. At the close I went forward, made a commitment of my life to this Jesus whom I tried to flee in the hospital, this Jesus who seemed to care about me although I did not understand why. That He would pursue me through Karen and through these intercessors astounded me, delighted me, overwhelmed me.

In recent years, the Lord has led me into a ministry to compulsive, addictive people that has taken me throughout our country and to other parts of the world. I am now able to give of myself as in the past I sought to receive. God has also given me the key to helping these people. *Prayer.* Some sharing and counsel, perhaps, but always steady, relentless, all-out, unremitting prayer, *with* them if possible and *for* them when I am alone.

God uses this kind of prayer to heal, to restore and to redeem the lost.

Will you take it upon yourself to reach out to despairing, hopeless people? Here are four suggestions:

1. Make your own list of desperate cases, those "most wanted ones—for the Lord."
2. Find appropriate Scriptures, and as you pray for these people, insert their names in the proper places.
3. Ask the Lord to help you overcome any unbelief you may have that these people can be healed and restored.
4. As you come against the enemy's power at work in these people, read Ephesians 6:10–20, with an awareness that having done all you can, you will "stand" and affirm the truth that *there are no hopeless cases.*

The Right Prayer at the Right Time

Joseph P. Bishop

Author of *New Beginnings*; former pastor of Rye Presbyterian Church; from Westerly, Rhode Island

Through my lifelong friendship with Annie, a woman crippled from birth with cerebral palsy, I learned many things, including this lesson in intercession:

One summer day years ago Annie asked me if I would drive her to Trenton where a famous preacher was having a healing mission. We were given a ticket admitting us to a special tent for people in wheelchairs and on stretchers.

Presently the pastor with the gift of healing came into the tent where I was sitting on the ground beside Annie's chair. Unquestionably, a power, a mighty force of some kind, entered with him. He moved from bed to chair, touching each person with vigor and claiming in the name of Jesus Christ that they were healed. When he left the tent, weeping and loud praising could be heard from all sides.

By my side Annie was straining to say something. It was hard to hear in the hubbub. "I want to walk," she said.

Eagerly I folded back the footsteps of the chair and helped her to her feet. Perspiring with the effort, she put one foot in front of the other. Then she grabbed my arm to steady herself as she backed into her chair again. Nothing was different. We were both struck dumb with disappointment.

"Let's go home," she murmured at last.

I pushed her chair over the dusty grass to the parking lot, and we drove home in almost total silence. Annie subsequently experienced one of the deepest depressions she had ever had.

Sometimes God's purpose can be thwarted by the wrong match between method and need. The approach does not fit the person. The answer is not the one intended for that problem at that time. In our enthusiasm to help, we often rush in with answers that have been effective in previous situations but are not appropriate to the one at hand.

What we should do is take time to find the Lord's launchpad rather than simply assume we know what it is. That was my mistake in taking Annie to Trenton; I never once stopped to pray for the leading of the Lord in the matter. The failure of the effort and the depression that followed were not the responsibility of the famous preacher whose gifts were authentic. The responsibilities were Annie's and mine.

The wisdom of waiting for the right prayer at the right time is something we learned some years afterward from Agnes Sanford. It was 1953 or 1954 when Agnes consented to come to Swarthmore, Pennsylvania, to conduct a healing mission in our church. From her wheelchair Annie looked up at Agnes and asked if Agnes believed the Lord was capable of healing her cerebral palsy through Agnes' prayers. Agnes responded with deep compassion that she did not have the faith for such a prayer. She would need time, she added, to discover how God wanted her to pray for Annie. Annie accepted that.

A year or so later Agnes returned to us for another mission. Annie was in the congregation. After the service the three of us went to my study together. Agnes went over to the window and stood looking at the white snowflakes still swirling about the light posts in the parking lot. At last she came to where we were waiting, Annie in her wheelchair, I perched on a corner of the desk.

"You know," Agnes began, "the Lord Jesus could do it, but I still can't believe for the healing of cerebral palsy. It would be like asking a tinker-toy engine to pull a Pennsylvania railroad train from Philadelphia to New York. I haven't the strength to channel that much power. But I do know what God desires for us tonight. He has given me the power to heal your urge for suicide."

Annie and I looked at each other, startled. I said, "Just yesterday Annie told me she wanted to die."

Agnes smiled. "There was a time when I could not go near a high window for fear of jumping out." She looked at Annie. "Do you want me to pray for you to be healed of this desire?"

Annie nodded. I knelt by her side while Agnes put her hands on Annie's head. She prayed about the rejection and frustration of Annie's past, and she asked the Lord to heal her desire for self-destruction.

Later Annie told me that as Agnes prayed for her, she felt a warmth flow through her "like a cup of hot, clear soup." There was a glowing radiance in the weeks and months that followed. A new beginning in Christ had come through the right prayer at the right time.

Agnes would not leave the window that snowy night until she received the Lord's specific guidance. She knew Jesus wanted to help Annie in some important, immediate way. Then it came to her: Annie had the urge to give up trying. That needed healing, and this was the moment for *this* specific, God-given intercession.

Only God knows whether or not Annie might still be healed of her physical affliction through some tremendous miracle. In the meantime, she has persevered from college to graduate work, to her doctorate, to employment, to research, to professional value and competence, to independence, to service for others, to witnessing for Christ in countless lives across the nation.

All this, thanks, at least in part, to an intercessor who had learned the wisdom in seeking the right prayer at the right time.

The Astonishing Power of One Mother's Prayers

Sondra Johnson

Communications director, Breakthrough; administrator, Christian Guidance and Counseling Center; from Hillsboro, Virginia

As a mother of four and stepmother of three, ages eleven to 28, I know only too well that feeling of helplessness when a child is exposed to the world's temptations and becomes too old for me to reach out physically and pluck him from danger. So I do what millions of other mothers have done through the ages. I lean upon prayer.

Some mothers do it better than others. One mother in particular is known worldwide for her diligent intercession. Her name was Monnica. I've studied her life, seeking her secret.

Monnica lived hundreds of years ago in an age when women were severely restricted. Her family-arranged marriage was to an unbeliever, a difficult man named Patricius who was given to frequent temper outbursts. They had two sons: The elder son, Augustine, was especially gifted, but independent-minded, rebellious, carnal.

Their family life, not too different from millions of families today, was turbulent. Monnica, a devout Christian, knew she was helpless in her own power to change her family, so she began intercession for them from the beginning.

How did Monnica go about it? Prayer every day, when alone, and twice each day in church.

It must have been terribly discouraging. Her husband seemed unwilling to change. Her son Augustine was in constant trouble. As a youth, he stole (even from his mother), he lied constantly, he got into fights. Though his mother patiently read him Scripture, taught him God's truths, he seemed completely uninterested in the Christian faith.

Monnica never lost hope. Her prayers just went deeper, with many tears. There seems to be something about a mother's tears that indicates relinquishment and reaches right to the heart of God. Augustine described it later in his life this way: "Out of my mother's heart's blood, through her tears night and day poured out, was a sacrifice offered for me to Thee."

The first breakthrough came with her husband. For years Monnica had suffered without complaint from his anger and verbal abuse, always praying for his salvation, being "reverently amiable." Her strategy was to pray, be patient and to show him Christ through her obedience and faithfulness. As a result, she won him to Christ. Patricius became a believer only months before his death, which came when their son Augustine was seventeen.

But by this time Augustine was in total rebellion. With his brilliant mind he sought the great philosophers, leaving home to go to school. "My spirit," he wrote, "was wholly intent on learning, and restless to dispute. I had my back to the light."

And then this: "Almost nine years passed, in which I wallowed in the mire of that deep pit, and the darkness of falsehood. . . . All of which time that chaste, godly, and sober widow . . . , no whit relaxing her weeping and mourning, ceased not at all hours of her devotions to bewail my case to Thee."

During this period, Augustine lived with a girlfriend (not the family's choice of a partner for him) and at nineteen fathered a son named Adeodatus. He continued to reject the Christian faith.

Augustine had a great love of the theater, which, when reading what he had to say about it, reminds me of the pornographic influence today of television on our young people. He described it this way: "Stage plays carried me away, full of images of my miseries, and of fuel to my fire . . . mine unpiety divided me against myself."

There was the occasion when Augustine, while living and teaching in Carthage, decided to sail to Rome where the allurements were great. Monnica had guidance from the Lord that this would be bad for him and stepped up her intercession, even following him to the seaport to protest his going. Augustine pretended to accept her decision, then slipped onto the boat and sailed away.

Monnica realized that prayer was her only hope, and she went back to her knees. In Rome, Augustine became deathly ill. "I felt," he said, "as if I was going down to hell, carrying all the sins which I had committed." But though he recovered, he did not change.

Monnica did not know what a close call her son had. She simply continued in her daily intercession. By now, however, she was turning to others for help. "I pray Thee will send the teachers Thee wants for my son," she begged the Lord.

Once when she asked a church leader to speak to Augustine and point out the error of his ways, the man turned her down, saying Augustine was "unteachable." Tearfully, Monnica continued to beg the man until he finally turned to her, saying ". . . God bless you. For it is not possible that the son of these tears should perish."

Later, when Augustine went to lecture in Milan, he became acquainted with Ambrose, the statesman bishop of that city. Because of Ambrose's influence, Augustine broke off his physical relationship with his woman companion. (She went on to join a religious community.) Augustine's plea became: "Give me chastity, but not yet."

Monnica's prayers, meanwhile, never abated.

And the warfare inside Augustine intensified. One day while talking with a friend, he unexpectedly burst into tears. Embarrassed, wondering if this was some kind of divine act, he returned to his house, picked up a volume of Paul's letters, opened it and was stabbed by these words:

"Not in rioting and drunkenness, not in chambering and wantonness, not in strife and envying; but put ye on the Lord Jesus Christ, and make not provision for the flesh, to fulfill the lusts thereof."

When Augustine revealed this episode to his mother, she rejoiced quietly. The answer to her prayers was near.

From then on there was a new peace in Augustine. Soon afterward he wrote to Ambrose, asking to be received as a convert. Ambrose baptized Augustine, at age 32, on Easter Sunday.

A year later Monnica, at age 56, took sick while traveling with her son and grandson Adeodatus. When asked if she feared death so far from her home, Monnica replied, "Nothing is far from God."

Several days later she died, her mission to her family completed.

Saint Augustine went on to become a bishop of the Church and one of the great leaders of the Christian faith. His writings have been compared to those of St. Paul. Throughout his famous book *Confessions*, Augustine credits his mother's prayers for his salvation. Indeed, she devoted her life to this cause.

Does any of us, when first beginning the adventure in motherhood, really realize that it will be a *lifetime* of prayer? The key factors in Monnica's intercession seem to be:

1. *Persistence*. Monnica prayed every day for her family.
2. *Church*. Monnica used the sacraments of her church, including Communion and confession. She was also very active in her church.
3. *Tears*. There was no holding back of her emotions. Her tears at times were a flood. They enabled her to relinquish her own desires for her family.
4. *Others*. Monnica sought the help and prayers of others, knowing that there was extra power in numbers.
5. *Trust*. Her trust was always in God. In His timing, in His power, in His love.

Rees Howells: Catalyst for a Miracle

Leonard LeSourd

Chairman of Breakthrough; former editor, *Guideposts* magazine; associate publisher, Chosen Books; from Lincoln, Virginia

Those of us who pray for others to be healed (James 5:14) can learn something from the amazing intercession work of Rees Howells, the Welsh coal miner. Rees never hesitated to pray for healings. But he depended totally on the Lord's direction as to the way he prayed.

How did a coal miner with limited education reach a spiritual level where he could hear the Lord's voice with regularity and obey it with certainty?

It came about because Rees had a hunger to know God and sought Him constantly through daily prayer. One day, at age 26, he heard this command: *Give your body to Me that I may work through it. It must belong to Me without reservation, for two persons with different wills can never live in the same body. If I come in as God, you must go out. I shall not mix My self with your self.*

Rees was stunned by this challenge of unconditional surrender—not unlike a sentence of death. He resisted for five days during which the contrast between the holiness of God and his own corrupt nature was starkly revealed. When Rees made the final surrender he was filled with the Holy Spirit and a ministry of power began. Shortly thereafter came one of the most difficult challenges of Rees' life.

Joe Evans, a dedicated helper and close friend, developed a severe case of tuberculosis. Doctors ordered him to a sanitorium. In agony of spirit, Rees sought the Lord for guidance. The answer came: *Let Joe follow medical advice.*

Five months in a sanitorium did not help, so the doctors suggested he try a tropial climate. "Was this right?" Rees asked the Lord. Again he was told to defer to the doctors.

Now Rees was faced with two dilemmas. First, Joe did not have the money to go to a warmer climate. Second, if the money was available, there was no one in Joe's family to accompany him.

Several days later, Rees received a gift of 320 pounds sterling for his work, more than enough to handle a trip for two to a tropical location. Rees had no trouble turning this money over to his friend, but who would go with Joe? The Lord's next direction was devastating: *Do not ask someone else to do what you can do yourself.*

New studies had shown that TB (Britishers called it consumption) was highly contagious. Since Rees was soon to be married, the possibility of contracting the disease filled him with horror. Yet did he have a choice? He and his fiancée agreed he did not.

In 1906 Rees Howells and Joe Evans traveled together to the island of Madeira in the Mediterranean. To save money, they stayed in a place called "The Sailor's Rest" provided by a Christian missionary. The food was terrible, vermin infested the place and the missionary was unfriendly.

Rees rebelled. "Lord, why this?" he prayed. There was no answer. Weeks passed and his anger toward the missionary grew. And there was no improvement in Joe. "I was tired and felt as if life wasn't worth living," Rees wrote in his journal. "I felt more like a man, than a man with the Holy Ghost inside me. I wanted to cry."

Rees was stricken. If the root of the Savior's nature was love, and if the root of his own nature was love, then nothing the missionary did could affect him. He was to love the missionary The change that then occurred in Rees was dramatic.

Meanwhile, Joe was getting worse in the tropical climate, with both lungs nearly eaten away by the disease. Rees was afraid Joe was about to die when one day the Lord whispered gently to him: *A month from today, Joe will be restored.*

With jubilation Rees reported the news to Joe, the missionary and other friends. They looked at Rees as if he had lost his mind. But having this positive word from the Lord, Rees went ahead with complete faith. Boat reservations were made for the return to England a month later. Joyous letters were written to both families. The doctors involved shook their heads in dismay.

Though Joe's condition was unimproved, excitement grew in Rees and Joe as the day approached. When it finally came, Rees expected the healing to take place at dawn. Nothing happened. Instead, the Lord told Rees to announce in advance the good news to families back home by telegram. Another test of his faith, but Rees obeyed.

At noon, Joe and Rees were sitting in front of their lodgings when the Lord came down on Joe like a shower of rain. He was healed. It was instantaneous—so complete that Joe began to jump about and dance. Then he asked Rees to run a race with him. Then another. It seemed that all the Lord's power had gone to Joe's legs. It was joy unspeakable. Soon thereafter the two men made a triumphant return to Great Britain.

There are numerous lessons to learn from this story:

1. The Lord uses doctors and often will not act until a case is beyond medical help.
2. We can be His instruments for healing if we are willing to pay the price of surrender, self-discipline and obedience.
3. As we begin to pray for others, God will often do an unexpected work inside us.
4. The Lord does the healing at His choice of time and place.
5. The key to power in intercession is to learn to hear God's voice and then obey it.

Why Are We Afraid to Believe in Miracles?

Lloyd J. Ogilvie

Senior pastor, First Presbyterian Church; author; host of the "Let God Love You" television and radio ministry; from Hollywood, California

The story of the apostle Peter's miraculous escape from the Jerusalem prison has a lot to teach us today about intercessory prayer.

This was a difficult time for the Christian church in Jerusalem. When King Herod discovered that the way to gain popularity and support from the Jews was to persecute Christians, he arrested James and had him beheaded. That brought him such acclaim that he had Simon Peter thrown into prison. Peter, like James, was to be beheaded.

The Jerusalem body of Christian believers was devastated at the loss of their leader—and at the precautions Herod took to prevent his escape. He ordered four squads to guard Peter. Since each squad contained four soldiers, that meant a total of sixteen guards for one spiritual leader who had broken no law.

There was nothing the church could do except pray. Nothing except pray? Many previously answered prayers should have told the Christians there is no more powerful weapon! But the passage in Acts tell us there were no bold prayers in the name of Jesus for Peter's release. They asked only that he be sus

207

tained and strengthened, somewhat surprising in the light of astounding answers to prayers all through Acts.

This story points up one of the great problems we all face: not so much how to pray, but what to pray. When a person we love is troubled, we are reluctant to be specific in our intercession because we fear telling God what we think best. We get into the muddle of what is our will versus what is God's will, as if the two could not be the same.

Years of trying to learn how and what to pray for others have taught me to spend more time listening to what the Lord wants me to ask than in asking. Then the asking can be what He is more ready to give than I may have had the courage to ask.

Discouragement over what we perceive as unanswered prayer in the past wilts our willingness to pray boldly. We assume that there was no answer because what happened was not what we wanted. Our limited view of time and eternity narrows our own perception of what an answer should be. Even after years of seeing God turn what we thought were problems into opportunities for good, we forget these experiences and get caught in judging what God will do in a present situation on the basis of what we thought He should have done previously, but didn't. This, perhaps, was what the church in Jerusalem was facing. "We prayed for James and he was beheaded," they said. "What else can we expect for Peter?"

Expectation is a crucial part of dynamic prayer. But it must be built on the insight and guidance of prolonged prayer to know how to pray. Building our prayers on unguided, negative expectations is disastrous. We expect far too little, we ask for it and then are disappointed that the Lord did not do better for us.

The formula for creative intercessory prayer is: Listen carefully, ask boldly, trust completely and know that the answer is part of the tapestry of God's greater plan. He uses everything for His glory and our growth, if we allow Him.

The Lord's timing of Peter's rescue was right on schedule. On the night before Herod was to execute Peter, an angel of the Lord appeared in the prison to set him free. The sleeping apostle did not wake easily. What a splendid picture of trust and serenity! The angel struck the apostle a smart blow on the side to move him from his confident sleep. Then he had to lead the sleeping saint each step of the way, giving instructions to him for putting on his sandals and robe. What is implied was that he was in a half-awake trance. The tall, robust fisherman was cared for like a little child.

What happened was a three-part miracle. The first part was to get Peter out of the chains, which were linked to the arms of the two guards; the second was to get him past the guard posts; and the third was to get him through the iron gate of the wall surrounding the whole prison. The angel accomplished all three without the guards' being roused. It was not until Peter and the angel were out of the prison and down the street that he fully woke up!

I think the whole company of heaven was watching that night. "The great cloud of witnesses," the heavenly cheering section, was pulling for the success of the event. And I think they laughed as Herod was outsmarted one more time. Also, it must have been a very humorous thing to see the church continuing to pray with little expectation while Peter was already out of prison!

Since Peter wanted to share the joy with his sisters and brothers in Christ, he made his way to the home where they were gathered, and knocked. When he announced himself, at first no one believed him.

When finally they opened the gate, the praying fellowship saw Peter and was astonished. As the news spread, *the Word of God grew and multiplied.*

This story says a lot to us in regard to our prayers:

1. Expectation is the gift we offer the Lord in response to His gift of prayer. It is what we bring as an offering for our communication with Him. Expectation is a blend of confident trust and sanctified imagination. It gives us the capacity to ask the Lord for what He wants to give.

2. The Lord answers all prayer. Knowing so much more than we do, He grants some, refuses others, and delays still others. A delay is an answer! To have what He wants for us without His timing would be disastrous.

3. Often the answer we have been praying for is staring us in the face. Sometimes the Lord responds with a portion of the answer, which requires joyous acceptance and implementation before we can appropriate the whole. We cannot receive the rest until we act on the first step.

4. There are times when we are so intent on praying that the prayer is all talking and no listening. Remember, the answer may be knocking!

X
Angelic Protection

When you pray for people in a crisis situation, or for loved ones about to take a trip, do you ask God to send them protecting angels? If you do not, you could be denying them something they desperately need.

You may say, "Why should I do that? God knows how to deal with these situations. I just pray to Him."

True, God is omnipotent and omniscient. Yet we are told in Scripture to pray specifically, to ask. And asking for angelic assistance may mean more than you could possibly realize.

Angels Watching Over You and Me

Betty Malz

Author of *My Glimpse of Eternity*
and other books; from Crystal
Beach, Florida

Did you pray today for angelic protection?

We are living in such dangerous times that we need every bit of protection a loving heavenly Father offers. My husband and I always begin the day asking God to protect us with the angelic force at His command. Also, when starting on a trip by car or plane, we ask for this help. Our prayers also seek special angelic covering for any of our children or grandchildren if they are embarking on travel or a difficult venture. That God will give us this help is affirmed throughout the Bible. Look at these examples.

When reading how Elijah prayed for assistance against four hundred and fifty false prophets, I like to imagine scores of angels in heaven bearing fiery torches receiving the command, "Go." The Bible tells us that fire poured out of the sky, consuming the sacrificial offering, thus enabling Elijah to destroy his enemies (1 Kings 18:38–40).

Later, when Elijah fled into the wilderness to avoid the wicked Queen Jezebel, he never left the Lord's protection. He had been obedient and the Lord did not forget him. An angel appeared with nourishment and jostled Elijah awake: "Arise, and eat." Elijah was fed cake and water in a parched and dry land and traveled for forty days on the strength of that one heaven-sent meal.

This account of the Old Testament prophet gives us at least three important directives for expecting angelic assistance. First, *be obedient*. If we enter an impossible situation through the Lord's leading, we can expect His hosts to defend us. Second, *be selfless*. If we are promoting a self-serving cause, we have no right to look for divine intervention. But if we are doing what God calls us to do, out of a motive of love and service to others, we can and should expect His special help. And third, *honor God*. This may be the most important principle of all. Aren't we supposed to love the Lord God with all our heart, soul, mind and strength?

And who could ever forget the story of Daniel who was thrown into a den of hungry lions because he refused to stop his worship of God, a capital offense in Babylon? The next day Daniel was alive and well and reported: "My God sent His angel and shut the mouths of the lions. They have not hurt me."

I do not believe the angel wrestled with the lions physically and muzzled them. I think the Lord sent the angel, saying: "Go, have a word with those lions." Then the angel dropped down, touched each one on the nose and said, "Don't you touch Daniel. He's the beloved of the Lord." The angel's authority caused the lions to submit. I personally believe those hungry lions would rather starve than disobey God's angel.

When the king of Babylon saw the miraculous results of the angel's intervention, he declared that the entire kingdom would worship the God whom Daniel served. Daniel had stood in the gap between danger and safety out of obedience to God, putting his life in the Lord's hands.

Nothing has changed in 2000 years regarding angelic protection, except there probably are more angels at work today. Our prayers set in motion the heavenly forces today as well.

Wyman Grosvenor and his wife, Claudia, found this out one Saturday night when they knelt beside their bed and felt "nudged" to pray for their daughter, Cindy. She was working at night as a waitress in one of the famous restaurants in the French Quarter of New Orleans, only three miles from her home.

At midnight closing time, their daughter left the restaurant and as she turned the corner walking toward the parking lot, two men grabbed her and flung her onto the brick floor of the alleyway. One man put his knee on her chest, choking her throat, while the other one wrenched her purse from her hand. She gasped, "Jesus, help!"

Suddenly into the dark alleyway appeared a very large man. The alley was illuminated though he did not carry a flashlight. With authority he asked, "Cindy, do you know these men?"

How did he know my name? she wondered.

The two men fled. The helper assisted her to her car, and when he released her hand she turned to thank him, but he was gone, vanishing as quickly as he had appeared.

Cindy locked her car doors, leaned back against the head rest and wept with shock and relief. While driving the three miles home, she struggled to keep calm, so fearful was she that the men would follow her and find where she lived. She dreaded turning off the ignition and walking down the driveway to the porch and the house.

When she pulled up in front of her home, she turned off the engine and opened the car door. Looking up, she saw her protector waiting. Again he took her hand and saw her safely to the door. When Cindy turned to say thanks, he was gone.

The Grosvenors told me this story when I spoke at a church near their home recently. Nothing at all unusual about this—I hear these types of stories wherever I go today. We are living in such an age of violence that I believe God's protecting angels are all about us as never before.

It is prayer that calls them to action. Two words can do it—"Jesus, help!" Or just the one-word prayer—"Jesus."

God's Special Helpers

Leonard LeSourd

Chairman of Breakthrough; former editor, *Guideposts* magazine; associate publisher, Chosen Books; from Lincoln, Virginia

Each Christmas we are reminded of the role angels played at the birth of Jesus. "An angel of the Lord appeared, saying, 'I bring you tidings of great joy' . . . suddenly a great company of the heavenly host appeared with the angel, praising God."

If we can accept the role of angels as Yuletide messengers, can we accept them now as God's special helpers in everyday intercession?

From all my study and experience with intercessory prayer, it seems obvious that angels serve as the Lord's indispensable agents for answering the prayer requests of His people. The Bible is filled with a hundred or more references to angels serving in this role.

Skeptical people wonder, "Are there enough angels to handle the prayer requests of people today?"

There are. The book of Revelation says: *And the number [of angels] was ten thousand times ten thousand, and thousands of thousands* (5:11, KJV). That's more than one hundred million angels praising Him around the throne! If God needs two billion angels today to serve His people, you can be sure He has them!

Others ask, "Why should God be concerned about the little problems of ordinary people?"

But He is. Scripture says so, that He even knows the number of hairs on the head of each person!

I was given some new insights about God's awesome knowledge and power in this respect when I dug in recently on the whole subject of intercession. I started with the dictionary and found this definition: *Intercession*—"A pleading with God in behalf of another or others." A concordance directed me to Hebrews 7:25.

The Hebrews passage (beginning with verse 24):

> Because Jesus lives forever, he has a permanent priesthood. Therefore he is able to save completely those who come to God through him, because he always lives to intercede for them.
>
> NIV

So we see Jesus as the Intercessor. He takes our case before God when we go to Him (also see Romans 8:26).

I looked up the Hebrews quotation in the *New Laymen's Bible Commentary* and came across this statement:

> How great to have Jesus as our High Priest and Intercessor seated in heaven; *for this unseen world is the real world*, a heavenly sanctuary, a magnificent permanent headquarters for the Intercessor.

It was as if a bell had gone off in my brain. *For this unseen world is the real world!*

How small our thinking is! Our world seems so big and all-important to us that we cannot begin to grasp the immensity of the heavenly kingdom. We talk about having to deal with reality, the real world of the here and now. God must smile at our pompousness. Our earth is but a speck in His cosmos and a brief experiment in His infinity.

Yet He loves each one of us, cradles us in His hands *and hears us!* Why not? In that real world of His, He has a tremendous, fabulous heavenly network—a communications system that would make our biggest and most complex computer look like a child's toy. And the messengers/helpers in this network are the countless millions of angels who can act in a split second if so needed.

Take the case of Jack and Jenny Pate of Galveston, Texas. They and their three-year-old daughter, Peggy, were in the upstairs room of their new home one warm summer day to do some wallpapering. The window was opened for ventilation. Peggy began playing among the wallpaper scraps, dropping little bits of paper from the upstairs window, watching as they were caught by the current of the breezes to flutter and swirl to the ground.

The sight so fascinated Peggy that she began to lean farther and farther over the sill.

Jack happened to look up at the very moment his little Peggy tumbled out the window.

"Jesus!" he shrieked.

Beneath the window was a cement patio with three concrete steps having sharp protruding corners leading up to the door of the house. The thought of their daughter's body striking hard concrete from a second-story window paralyzed both Jack and Jenny with horror.

Then together they almost exploded down the stairs to reach the crumpled little body. Sobbing, they burst through the front door.

There, sitting on one of the concrete steps, her little hands folded in her lap, was Peggy. Looking up, she softly whispered, "Don't worry. That big man caught me."

Dumbstruck, they hugged their child, saw with joy and relief that she was unhurt, then looked about to thank the man who had saved their daughter. It was an open-country area and he could not have gone far. But there was no one in sight!

The whole family talked of nothing else for some time, marveling, speculating. Nonbelievers were convinced that the "man" who caught Peggy had for some reason disappeared.

The others believed the answer lay in Isaiah 63:9: "The angel of His presence saved them."

There was only a split second between the one-word prayer "Jesus!" and the arrival of the angel. The Pates certainly have no questions about God's supernatural ability to answer our prayers through His helpers.

Nor does anyone in our family, especially after an experience we had back in 1969. Catherine and I and our two teenage sons, Chet and Jeff, were driving from the north to our home in Boynton Beach, Florida. Before we started we prayed for spiritual protection on the trip as we always did. The trip was made without incident. We arrived at our home on a scorchingly hot, September afternoon. After unpacking the car, the two boys seemed about to jump into the pool for a swim, as they usually did. Instead they went to their rooms to relax as I began checking things around the house.

When dusk came, I started to turn on the switch for the underwater light in our small swimming pool. The light always created a beautiful glow on the patio. But I made a disturbing discovery. The pool light switch was already in the "on" position. Obviously the light had burned out.

Or—and then a prickly feeling crept through my body. Could the light have shorted out from the water somehow? If so, the pool water could be dangerously electrified.

Quickly I put the switch in the "off" position and taped it over, warning the rest of the family not to touch it. Then I reviewed all that I knew about pool lights. Special legislation had been passed several years before, ruling out pool lights underwater unless they were enclosed in a special watertight unit that guaranteed their being leak-proof. But nothing could be done about pool lights installed before this legislation was passed unless individual pool owners took the necessary action. I had no idea what kind of pool light had been installed in our pool because we had purchased our home from another couple several years after it had been built.

An electrician was called. He came, checked the pool light

carefully, then summoned me with a very sober look on his face.

"How long had the switch been in the 'on' position?"

"I don't know."

"Nobody went swimming, obviously."

"Not that I know of."

" 'Twould have been too bad if they had."

"You mean the pool was electrified?"

"Had to be. Water leaked into the light socket and shorted out the circuit. The current then soaked the pool water. We've had too many deaths from this sort of thing. I've disconnected the circuit. Don't ever try to reconnect it without getting a whole new unit."

Shocked, I called the family together and asked Chet and Jeff why they had not plunged into the pool the moment they got home as they ordinarily did.

They looked puzzled. "For some reason we just decided to lie down instead of jumping into the pool," said Chet. "I don't know why."

Stunned by such a close call, we gathered together for a prayer of thanksgiving. At that point I became convinced that God honored these prayers for protection in a supernatural way. From then on each time any member of our family began a trip by auto, I visualized a protecting angel "riding shotgun" while sitting on the front bumper.

Previously, I had been somewhat skeptical about angel stories—the unseen hand that wrenched the steering wheel a certain way to avoid a crash; a sudden and mysterious pressure on the brake to slow down a car before the driver was aware of the crisis situation ahead; the driver who claimed he actually saw an angel stop a car that was careening out of control down a hill. I am now convinced that the spiritual warfare that goes on in the unseen world is becoming more intense and building to a climax.

The steps to seek supernatural help in your prayers of intercession are simple:

1. Believe that God has a vast army of angelic forces that He calls upon for our help and protection.

2. Make the prayer specific, such as: "Lord, please send Your protecting angels to be with Charlie today as he drives home from Detroit."
3. Visualize one or more angels "riding shotgun" on the car or the wings of a plane or whatever.
4. When a trip or venture has been safely completed, give God a thanksgiving offering.

On a Road in the Middle East

Deborah Strong

Missionary in the Philippines

Late one night I was walking along a road in the Middle East. I had just been at a meeting and was on my way home. The night was still and quiet, and I was enjoying some much-needed private moments with my Jesus. Suddenly, a group of eight men jumped out from behind a low wall. Encircling me, they blocked my path on the narrow dirt road. I looked around quickly for help but no one was in sight or earshot.

I do not know that I could have screamed for help anyway. My vocal cords, along with the rest of me, were paralyzed with fear. I wish I could say that I was a woman of great faith and power. The truth is, I was just plain scared.

Reality hit me full force. These men could not care less that I was a missionary in their country on God's mission. I was a fair-skinned, blue-eyed, blonde foreign woman . . . not a very good thing to be on that dark, lonely road.

With arms folded across their chests and legs slightly spread and firmly planted, each man leered at me out from under his white turban. I glanced from one face to another seeking mercy. They just stared back at me, unmoving.

A thought blasted into my mind: *This is not fair. God's got lots for me to do yet. I can't die now.*

Then words from the Bible rose up within me loud and clear: "Greater is He who is in you than he who is in the world. No weapon formed against you shall prosper. *God's Word never fails.*" As soon as His Word came to me, that immobilizing fear vanished. I mean simply vanished into thin air as a righteous anger flooded me and a holy boldness swept through me.

Staring at one of the men, the one who seemed to be the leader, I said to him, "Out of my way, please." Nothing happened. He just smiled crudely back at me and chuckled. All the others joined in. Their laughter was enough to cause the hairs on my arms to stand straight up.

Then it dawned on me that they did not understand English. I was trying to think of a way to communicate in sign language when I remembered suddenly that there is a name that knows no language barriers. I pointed my finger right in the man's face and commanded him, "In the name of Jesus, let me go through."

This man looked around sheepishly at his companions, laughed nervously and smiled ever-so-slightly at me. I smiled back. Then he bent at the waist and, with his right arm extended, made a wide, sweeping bow, motioning me by him. I squeezed in between him and the man next to him and began to walk away slowly.

Everything within me was screaming *run* but I knew instinctively that for my life's sake, I should just walk. I somehow knew if I ran they would be after me. When I was about twenty feet away, curiosity overcame me, and I glanced back over my shoulder.

A strange sight greeted my eyes. Not one of the men had moved a millimeter! Their arms were still crossed on their chests and their legs were still spread and planted in the same position. They were looking at each other, but were not speaking. I sensed the reason they had not moved was because they could not. I had a vision of angels on the scene, grasping with iron grips, holding them in place.

I continued to walk slowly to the nearest turn in the road.

Finally, after what seemed an eternity, I was around the corner. Then I ran for my life!

"Thank You, God, thank You," I whispered, shaking all over.

But that is not the end of the story. A month later I received a letter from a friend back in the U.S. She had been awakened one night with a vision in which she saw me walking along a road alone. Then, unexpectedly, several tall, concrete-like pillars encircled me. Sensing that I was in great danger, my friend began to intercede on my behalf. Over and over she said, "Greater is He who is in you than he who is in the world. No weapon formed against you shall prosper." As she continued praying, this vision changed before her. A shaft of light hit one of the pillars, toppling it. As it fell, she saw me walking out on the shaft of light to safety.

She wrote me at once to find out what had happened to me that night: It was the same night I faced those turbaned men!

XI
Intercessors in Action

Though devoted to the lonely work of praying for others, many of whom they do not know, intercessors are sometimes called to action. It may be to take a prayer walk in their own neighborhoods by the homes of hurting people or to go to an embattled city or country or to help the poor and homeless or to assist a person hurt in an accident.

Whatever the need, the intercessor has the necessary equipment for any adventure in faith—prayer.

Emergency Prayer

Peggy Sparks

Prayer warrior; from Austin, Texas

It was a hot August afternoon in 1979. As I drove down the street in my hometown of Austin, Texas, I saw a crowd gathered about an accident. Two high school students on a motorcycle had been hit by a big car. One boy apparently had a broken collarbone, ribs and other injuries, but was conscious. The second boy had had the lower part of his left leg crushed. Blood was pouring down the street and into the sewer opening. He was in shock and obviously bleeding to death.

Meanwhile, no ambulance or law enforcement people had arrived. The onlookers did not seem to know what to do. None of us, I guess, was medically trained to give first aid.

I stopped at the curb, got out of my car and ran over to the badly injured boy. I had on a floor-length dress, which I spread out, shielding him from the hot sun. Then I found myself raising my arms to the heavens and praying loudly in tongues. As I did so large tears poured out of my eyes onto his face. The crowd made not a sound. After five minutes or so the Lord bade me to stop praying.

Soon the ambulance arrived and took the two boys to the

hospital. The one who had lost so much blood seemed near death.

A woman stopped me on the way to my car and asked, "Was that your son or someone you know?" I said, "No, I was just praying."

She looked as though she thought I was real stupid to do that. I felt I had only done what the Lord wanted. Later I was pleased to learn that the badly injured boy had not died.

Two months later I was in a car with two lady friends. We were on our way to an early morning prayer breakfast. As we passed the place of the accident I told them how I had been led to pray for the two boys.

One of my friends yelled out, "Now I know why he didn't die!"

It had been her nephew who was hurt so badly. When the doctors opened up the boy's upper leg, they found that the main artery and blood vessels had been totally severed. He should have bled to death, but they found—as the doctors described it—that it appeared as if a giant pair of fingers had pinched off the flow of blood from both ends. This had saved him from bleeding to death. In fact, they had to cut open the ends of the blood vessels to join them back together.

There was no way that I could have known how to pray or what to pray for. As I stood over him and prayed and shed those large tears, a power seemed to take charge. I have never experienced anything like that before or since. Afterward, not my eyes or nose or mouth had the appearance of my having been crying. Only the Holy Spirit knows how to minister like this.

Intercessor at Work

Nate Larkin

Pastor; from Pompano Beach, Florida

At seven o'clock in the morning, Ferdinand Mahfood is at his desk, working as the proprietor of an exporting company in Pompano Beach, Florida. He has already spent an hour and a half in prayer.

Ferdinand—known simply as "Ferdi" to his many friends—is also the founder of Food for the Poor, Inc., which has collected and shipped more than twelve million dollars in privately donated food, bedding, building materials and other necessities to churches in the slums and villages of Haiti and Jamaica.

Ferdi Mahfood is also an intercessor.

Mahfood's spiritual odyssey began in 1975 when his wife, Patty, gave him a copy of Catherine Marshall's book *Something More*. Ferdi was finishing the final chapter while on flight to Chicago when he had an experience that he still remembers with startling clarity: "As I sat there reading, somehow the Holy Spirit came out of the pages of that book and came into my body. Tears started to run out of my eyes like a river. I started to pray. I was overcome by a power much greater than I."

Today, the holy sense of awe remains. Ferdi spends two hours each day in prayer, much of it in silence. He says that, for him, prayer and silence belong together—that prayer is communion with God during which two-way communication happens. "I quiet myself so that He prays, not me," he states. "The Bible says that the Holy Spirit knows how to pray in a way that we don't. So I pray that the Holy Spirit would use me as a vessel, that He would pray to the Father through Jesus Christ, and that I would sit down and shut up.

"What I take to God in my heart," Ferdi explains, "is what He sees. If I pray for you, I put you inside my heart, take you to God and God sees you in there. I don't have to say anything. He knows." His eyes become misty. "This morning, as I finished praying and I opened my eyes, I just cried. You reach a point where there's nothing to say."

Ferdi maintains that intercession is the source of his apparently endless supply of energy. Once he has left his prayer-closet, his office becomes a virtual whirlwind of activity, with Ferdi calmly at its center. He carries in his heart the needs of nine million people, many of them hungry and homeless. He writes, speaks, phones and cajoles on their behalf, doing his best to meet the urgent requests of the missionaries, pastors and priests who serve them. The resources of his company are donated to the mission, making it possible for Ferdi to deliver 95 cents of every dollar directly to Haiti or Jamaica in the form of aid. When asked to define his mission, he says simply: "God has called me to beg for the poor."

Standing in the Gap for Coalinga

Richard Schneider

Senior staff editor, *Guideposts* magazine; from Rye, New York

Lois Main, a middle-aged wife and mother who lives in Coalinga, California, returned home from a religious retreat on April 30, 1983, with a strong inner call to intercessory prayer.

At the retreat she had learned that an intercessor is one who stands in the gap between man and God, making requests before God on behalf of others. God seemed to be telling her that this was to be her ministry.

This bothered Lois. "I wasn't too sure that I wanted to be that involved," she admitted later.

Sunday, May 1, dawned bright and clear in this San Joaquin valley town of 7,000 people. But despite the beautiful weather Lois Main awakened feeling strangely oppressed. When she went to the Coalinga Believers' Church, she met several women who felt the same way. At evening services the women continued to pray for a lifting of this oppression.

Before retiring that night, Lois sat down to read the Bible. She could not concentrate, so went to bed. The inner tension was stranger than ever. Words were implanted on her mind:

Pray for the people of Coalinga. . . . Go out and pray for My children now.

"Yes, Lord." Lois climbed out of bed, dressed, walked out into the starlit night. Except for her soft footsteps, the town was still. Looking up beyond the hills, she prayed softly: "O Lord, protect the people, watch over the children."

She walked through the dark streets of Coalinga, praying for the residents of each house she passed. She passed the Service Pharmacy, Petty's Jewelry, State Market, now all quiet and dark, and then walked west to the Pleasant Valley Estates subdivision. Since Coalinga is above the San Andreas rock fault, she prayed for protection from an earthquake.

As the stars began to fade, Lois Main finally felt released from her prayer assignment. Legs aching and deeply fatigued, she returned home and slipped into bed at 5:30 A.M.

Monday was another beautiful day as Coalinga bustled into activity; children trotted off to school, autos and pickups filled the streets and merchants prepared for Mother's Day shoppers. Then at 4:42 P.M. the earth shivered and shook as the rock fault underneath exploded.

The earthquake, registering at 6.5 on the Richter scale, was one of the largest in our nation's history. It reverberated throughout most of southern California and as far east as Reno, Nevada.

Coalinga was especially hard hit. In the Service Pharmacy, nineteen-year-old Gina Lipe was racing toward the side entrance when a brick wall above her crumbled. Suddenly, for Gina, everything turned black.

Wanda Young was in Petty's Jewelry when the walls swayed and then closed in on her. "O God," she prayed, "please give me a tunnel out of here!"

Inside the State Market, Marie King stood paralyzed by fear as mustard jars and glassed condiments crashed around her. Almost fainting, she felt strong arms encircle her from behind and a calm voice saying: "Marie, I will steady you so you won't get hurt."

Timbers shrieked and bricks thundered to the street as buildings crumbled into rubble. But amid it all, unbelievable things happened.

A UPS driver saw Gina Lipe buried by the falling brick wall, called to some men and together they dug her out. Her injuries? A broken finger.

In Petty's Jewelry, Wanda Young's prayed-for tunnel had opened up, formed by wedged fallen beams, and she had picked her way safely to the street.

Inside the State Market, Marie King stared in amazement as the final shock subsided. The floor was knee deep in a shattered glass ooze of mustard, catsup and relish, except for a three-foot clear space all around her. The person behind her had released his hold and when she turned around to thank him, there was no one there.

At the hospital, doctors, who had rushed to gear up for an expected onslaught of victims, were probably the first to realize that a miracle had taken place. Instead of an onslaught of victims, only 25 people showed up, and most of them for minor injuries.

Lois Main and her family? This little group cowered under their stairway at home as blocks and debris pounded at the closed bedroom door behind them. Lois usually left that door open, but for some reason that afternoon she closed it. The sturdy oaken door shielded them. When the family finally escaped to the street after the final shock, they looked back at the house in awe. Only one wall remained.

In the days that followed, Coalingans began to learn of Lois Main's prayers for them. And not just Lois. Two other women, Ruth Long and Marilyn Tarvin, had been obedient to the same mysterious, urgent message to "Pray for My people."

Today, Coalingans are busily rebuilding their homes and businesses. Lois Main and her family have just recently moved into their new home built on the site of the old one destroyed by the quake.

Though she and her family have lost much materially, "We have all learned a lot about intercessory prayer," she says.

Burden for Our Nation's Capital

Barbara Melin

Writer; from Edina, Minnesota

Four intercessors from Minnesota had a burden for the nation's capital in March 1988 and did something about it. Dorothy, Diane, Dee and myself felt called to leave our families and drive to Washington, D.C., in my gray Toyota to engage in spiritual warfare there—an advance force for the great gathering on April 29, Washington for Jesus '88.

Before the journey began we received word that the angels would go before us, that the car would be our throne room and that the Lord would instruct us along the way.

As we approached Washington, we read again the biblical account of how Joshua took the walled city of Jericho by marching around it seven times. The last time around the trumpet was sounded, the walls fell down and Joshua's forces captured the city.

After checking into our motel in Crystal City, Virginia, two miles from D.C., we decided to do a "Jericho march" by car around Washington's beltway once each day we were there, a 64-mile "march." As we drove we prayed for the sins of our nation, for the apathy of the people. Then we broke into songs of praise, sounding as trumpets clarioning a call through the night, in the Spirit, to those who had ears to hear.

Each morning in Washington we received in our quiet time numerous Scriptures, like this one from 2 Chronicles 20:15–17: "This is what the Lord says to you: 'Do not be afraid or discouraged . . . the battle is not yours, but God's. Tomorrow march down against them. . . . Take up your positions; stand firm and see the deliverance the Lord will give you' " (NIV).

And so it went for seven days. The Lord gave us Scriptures in the morning, we covered different parts of Washington during the day; in the evening came the 64-mile drive around the beltway.

We encountered fierce spiritual warfare everywhere, especially while walking seven times around the new Russian Embassy (did they have us under surveillance?).

On the third day we discovered an Islamic Center on Massachusetts Avenue, so we took authority there. Then we traveled down Pennsylvania Avenue to the White House, past the Department of Treasury and Old Executive Office Building—all circled seven times.

One day as we circled the Capitol building, we were given this Scripture for our elected officials:

> The acts of the sinful nature are obvious: sexual immorality, impurity and debauchery; idolatry and witchcraft; hatred, discord, jealousy, fits of rage, selfish ambition, dissensions, factions and envy; drunkenness, orgies, and the like. I warn you, as I did before, that those who live like this will not inherit the kingdom of God.
>
> Galatians 5:19–23 (NIV)

On one of our Jericho drives around Washington, Dee had a vision of two angels hovering over the city, unfurling what looked like a blanket of the Spirit, rolling lightly as a protective shield over the city, against the demonic hosts.

One day we went to three hearings that we found listed in *The Washington Post*. One was on the inequities of the IRS penalty codes, another was on narcotics, in the third, Secretary of State George Schultz was appearing before the Foreign Relations Committee for the INF Treaty. Fasting and prayer through all of this left each of us wrung out from the warfare in the Spirit.

On our final day we met with a friend, Nita Scoggin, at the Pentagon while she led a Bible study of 27 women who work there. Afterward we listened, fascinated, while Nita confirmed everything that had happened to us all week. She told of attempts to bomb the Pentagon, and shared her view that we are a nation on the verge of disaster unless enough intercessors rise up to save us.

We drove back to Minnesota, exhausted but triumphant. We had been obedient, had given our all. The results were not our business, only the Lord's.

When Your Flight Is Canceled

B. J. Funk

> Prayer warrior; co-author of *Divorced, I Never Thought It Could Happen to Me*; from Chula, Georgia

I was on my way to a conference on intercessory prayer. For months, I had anticipated this trip, but I had some real fears—flying, the vastness of the airports, finding my way around.

Though friends and I had been praying for the conference and for my flight for weeks, my fears, resting somewhere at the bottom of my stomach, first began to flutter when my 9:30 A.M. flight out of Atlanta was cancelled due to mechanical difficulties. Forty minutes later, seated in a new plane and buckled in for takeoff, we were informed that this plane, too, had some mechnical problem and we would have to be reassigned. All around me were moans and expressions of anger. The tiny knot of fear in my stomach began to swell.

As I walked back into the airport feeling very alone, I heard loud, angry words: "This airline will hear from me!" The woman standing behind me continued her displeasure at the attendants. She was not the only one voicing her wrath.

In the midst of the commotion around me, I felt a quiet confidence settling in. I knew the feeling; recognized it from years of praying for strangers. God was giving me a job to do.

And so I prayed for the people around me, especially the loud, angry woman. "Lord, help this woman. Calm her. Bless her. Bring her to know You in a deeper way."

I was soon told there would be no way I could fly into Dulles airport—my intended destination outside of Washington, D.C. I would have to wait two more hours and fly into Washington's National airport, some 25 miles from Dulles. New concerns arose.

But before I could fully bemoan the setbacks, a sense of expectancy covered me. I had already seen God moving through these circumstances to bring about prayer for several people I did not know. What else did He have in mind? I felt confident He was in control.

As I waited at my departure gate, a young man sat down by me, his pleasant manner soon allowed me to share some of my new concerns. I am sure to that seasoned traveler (an FBI agent) all my fears seemed extremely minor, but he reacted with kindness, assuring me that everything would be just fine. His gentle confidence gave me a boost.

On boarding the plane, I discovered I had been given a delightful surprise. Because of my two cancelled flights, I had been moved to First Class on this new plane. Special treatment! The airline's way of making up for the inconvenience. But to me, God's way of showing He is always at work in my life.

My seat partner turned out to be a Christian. He and I enjoyed uplifting talk the entire flight. As we made our way to the luggage ramp, I saw a familiar face in the crowd—the kind FBI man who had sat with me before boarding.

Both men had their luggage by now, but mine was nowhere to be seen. The FBI man led me to a small room where I began filling out a claim form. He stood nearby, his somber expression and patrolling eyes indicating a man worthy of his vocation. His rigid stance made it appear that he was my bodyguard. A sense of God's presence poured over me.

Another familiar face appeared. It was the angry woman I had prayed for in Atlanta! Her luggage had also been lost, but now she was laughing and talking with me. Why had this woman reentered my life? Perhaps it was to encourage me concerning my prayers for her.

At last I reached my destination. I arrived just thirty minutes before the conference was to start; exactly six hours after I should have arrived. But those hours had been filled with so much of the reality of God's tender care that I wouldn't have missed any of them!

And how appropriate that I would be attending meetings to learn more about intercessory prayer. After all, I had just seen firsthand the results of my intercession and the results of others interceding for me. And I carried with me the privilege of continuing to pray for my "fellow travelers." For there is no way they can be called strangers. Each of them made me more aware of the presence of God. He brought them into my path and into my heart, and now they will be a part of me forever.

Three Miles with the Lord

Leonard LeSourd

Chairman of Breakthrough;
former editor, *Guideposts* magazine; associate publisher, Chosen Books, from Lincoln,
Virginia

Walking early in the morning is a great time to pray for
family, neighbors, your community. To walk and pray any time
of the day energizes the body, stimulates creativity and nour-
ishes the spirit as you reach out to people.

Thursday afternoon, September 16, 1987, fifteen of us from
the National Prayer Summit conference started out on a three-
mile walk through the heart of Washington, D.C. We were
divided into groups of two, three or more. Each of us had a
map and some guidelines:

- No chitchat; pray without ceasing (1 Thessalonians 5:17);
- Be ready to intercede for people along the way as well as
  for those in government buildings;
- Come against strongholds, dark powers and principalities
  in the name of Jesus;
- Keep asking the Holy Spirit how and for whom to pray.

My wife, Sandra, Joy Dawson of Youth With A Mission and
I made up one group. We interceded for about twenty agencies. The Lord answered our requests for guidance all along the
way. There were surprises:

We began at the State Department Building at 23rd and D Streets. "What are we to pray for here, Lord?"

Come against the stronghold of deception.

As we prayed, all three of us saw clearly that the ways of international diplomacy are not the ways of Jesus who stands for truth, mercy, compassion, a willingness to be vulnerable.

Heading west toward Pennsylvania Avenue, our next major stop was in front of the Old Executive Office Building. As we paused before this formidable structure (a fortress of intellectualism) the word we received was *pride*.

In front of the White House we stood for some time interceding for the President and the staff. Then we were led to ask for them *Courage in taking moral stands. Resistance to the spirit of fear.*

At the Treasury Department building we felt deep conviction about our nation's debt. How far we have come from that scriptural warning, "Owe no man any thing . . ." (Romans 13:8, KJV)!

The National Theatre was not on our list of buildings to cover in prayer, but as we passed it, there were strong inner nudges to stop. God's guidance: Instead of being a place to proclaim truth, the stage and film businesses have become centers of carnality, blasphemy, homosexuality. *Come against the strongholds of obscenity and perversion,* we were told.

A man with a scruffy red beard, soiled sports shirt, shorts and tattered loafers walked by us, carrying a sack over his shoulder. He paused by the pay phone to check for abandoned coins, then stopped to rummage through the trash container, inserting bits of debris into his sack. How to pray for this street person whom we did not get the guidance to approach?

"Lord, heal him of bitterness and despair. Lead him to a mission where he can be fed and clothed."

In front of the Justice Department we were given this Scripture: "Let justice roll down like waters and righteousness like an ever-flowing stream" (Amos 5:24, NAS). We interceded for those men and women in the Department who were taking a stand against pornography.

The National Archives building has been the focal point of controversy recently. Inside is documentation of the courage and greatness of Americans, but also cruelty against Indians, Blacks, Mexicans, etc., we would like to forget. Some people want to see these records of our dark side destroyed. The Lord's strong reply: *Americans have committed grievous sin in the past for which My people need to confess and repent.* Using Daniel's example (Daniel 9) we acted as intercessors, confessed the sins of our people and repented for them.

Positive "vibrations" as we passed the Botanical Gardens. God's lovely creation was everywhere. A time of praise and rejoicing for this spot of beauty in the middle of the city.

Awesome to stand before the Capitol and consider 200 years of American history. The day before we had gathered in a small chapel inside to pray for our senators and representatives, led by Senate Chaplain Richard Halverson. Key insight here for our leaders: *The fear of the Lord is the beginning of wisdom.*

Our last stop was the Supreme Court, scene of much intercession in the past year. Believing that the Court decision for abortion had turned their building into a Jericho, one group of Christians had conducted what they called a "Jericho march" about the building (Joshua 5:13–6:21). More than thirty local churches had been involved in "four-hour prayer watches."

As Sandra, Joy and I prayed, we were given Psalm 33:13–15 for the nine Supreme Court justices: "The Lord looks from heaven; He sees all the sons of men . . . He understands all their works" (NAS). Then these words: *When they render their decisions from now on, may these nine justices tremble in body, spirit and mind as they face their accountability before God and the time when they stand before the Heavenly Throne of Judgment.*

The walk through the heart of Washington took us two hours and twenty minutes. At the end we felt rejuvenated, refreshed and ready to do it again. And more in love with America than ever, perhaps because we felt newly involved in the workings of our government. The Lord had given us some of His feelings toward America, too . . . how much He loves this land He made, how He aches over our sinfulness, but also how He rejoices when His people bow before Him to confess their error, repent over their sins, sing praises to Him for His creation and then serve as His disciples.

An Orchid for Mary

Sandra Simpson LeSourd

Author of *The Compulsive Woman*; from Lincoln, Virginia

I came out of the flower shop that Mother's Day feeling a bit sheepish. In my hands were two corsage boxes, not just the one I had intended to buy for my husband's mother.

"You never know who might enjoy that extra flower," I said in answer to Len's quizzical glance as I got into the car.

We drove to the Maryland nursing home where his 93-year-old mother, Lucile LeSourd, lay in a comatose state. The elevator door opened onto the fourth floor. The nursing home smells and sounds—even in this beautifully decorated place—jolted us to the reality of where we were. Several Alzheimer's patients sat in their wheelchairs. Some stared off into another time, a few called out angrily, flailing shrunken arms at imagined foes.

Len's mother lay motionless beneath a maroon knitted blanket. Her pale wrinkled face never moved when Len and I leaned down to kiss her. As Len talked to the motionless form, I slipped out of the room, picking up the extra corsage as I left.

At the nurses' station I asked if there was anyone on the floor who had no visitors. A tall nurse nodded vigorously, "Go see

Mary in 4–G. She's ninety-six and a love. Has no living rela-
tives."

In 4–G the sun was streaming in on a scene I found startling.
Seated in a green upholstered chair was an enormous woman.
Perched on top of her head was a Boston Red Sox baseball cap
under which sprang long tendrils of white cotton candy hair,
falling far past her shoulders.

"Mary, my name is Sandy," I said self-consciously. "I've
come to pay you a Mother's Day visit."

"OOOOOOh-EEEEE!" she boomed in a basso profundo. "Sit
down, child. Delighted you came to see an old reprobate like
me."

As I moved a red ottoman close to her chair, Mary's gnarled
hands fingered the folds of the bright polyester quilt that covered much of her torso. Her moon face and bulbous red nose
gave her the appearance of a kindly Mrs. Santa.

My eyes turned to the foot of her bed where rested a needlepoint picture of a nurse with Mary's name appliqued on it.

"My friends gave me that needlepoint after I retired from
fifty-five years of nursing," she offered proudly. "Nursing was
my life. . . . What did you say your name was?"

I murmured my name, but she never stopped talking. "Our
family had a dairy farm not far from Boston. . . ." Her eyes
filled suddenly with tears. "And I was always patching up the
animals. Some nights I'd stay till dawn with a sick cow. I
wanted to be a nurse since I was a little girl. My dad said they'd
find a way to send me to nursing school. How they did it I'll
never know.

"My two sisters were real pretty. They got married right out
of high school. There weren't many boys interested in a big
moose like me. Nope, I was never pretty, but I had good teeth."

She brushed a wisp of her fine white hair up under the visor
of her baseball cap. "I never married and had children of my
own, but I've loved little ones and big ones. You'd be surprised
how many said to me, 'Mary, I wish you were my mother!' "

Her watery gaze moved toward the window. She seemed to
be tiring. I sensed it was time to wind up my visit. Then came
a prodding inside me.

"Mary, do you know the Lord Jesus?"

"I dunno. Maybe so."

I drew a deep breath. "He loves you just like you love the ones you nursed."

"He does?" Her eyes filled with tears.

Then very quietly I asked if she would like to give her life to the Lord.

When she nodded, I led her through the steps. . . .

Soon it was time to leave. "Before I go, Mary, I have something for you. It's a yellow orchid corsage. Would you like me to pin it on you?"

Her eyes flooded with tears as she cradled the plastic container in her hands. The flower looked so fragile, so jewel-like.

"Oh, no," she said, "It's much too lovely to wear. Let me just hold it and look at it."

She raised the crystalline box into the fading sun's rays. The dainty orchid seemed lit from within by an unseen light. "It's so beautiful . . . it makes my heart hurt," she whispered. "How can I ever thank you?"

"Mary, it's you who have blessed me." I hugged her and kissed her moist cheek.

Weeks later, the door to Room 4–G was slightly ajar. I opened it gently and walked into the darkened room. The gold drapes were closed now, but for a small crack. Mary was breathing with obvious difficulty. The long white cotton hair was a tangle on her pillow. Her large frame seemed shrunken.

"Mary?" I called softly. "It's me, Sandy, your Mother's Day friend."

Her eyes flickered open for a moment and closed again. Mary was dying of uremic poisoning and was semi-conscious, the nurse told me.

As I reached down to give her a final good-bye kiss, my eyes fell upon the table at the foot of her bed. A shaft of light, slipping through the crack in the drapes, rested on a shining object. A plastic box. Inside a yellow ribbon anchored to a withered tendril of a flower.

It was her orchid. On top of a new Bible.

XII
God at Work in
Our Lives

All of us involved with intercession know that our assignment is to pray and leave the results to the Lord. Yet . . . yet we always wonder: What happened? Did anything happen?

At the Breakthrough prayer ministry we often never know the results, but on numerous occasions we do. Those requesting prayer have often had wonderful, surprising answers that they have sent on to us.

When such letters arrive, we rejoice. And when we pass them on to the readers of our newsletter, they rejoice, too.

We hope the following results lift your spirits as they have ours.

1. Father-Daughter Conflict

There has been a miraculous healing between my husband and my daughter. He had disowned her when she married seven years ago and would not see her. Last year I asked for prayer for a healing between them. Right when it was least expected by any of us, my husband suddenly went to see our daughter and made up with her completely.

There is no explanation for this but prayer. And the healing has been total. By that I mean my husband and my daughter are closer than ever before. There is no strain with us now, no fear of saying the wrong thing. The miracle God performed is so great; it's like the last seven years never happened.

As a result of this reconciliation, other great things have happened. I have been healed of arthritis. This disease came, I'm sure, because of a root of bitterness in me. I've also been delivered from a deep depression. The lessons and strengths I have gained through all this came through pain, but are priceless.

2. Battling Suicide

I had left Christianity and the church behind twice. My early life had been full of heartache, including the suicide of my mother and the loss of four babies who were stillborn and one who lived just a day.

Then my marriage situation was getting worse all the time. Though my husband, Bill, and I loved each other, circumstances of his work kept us apart most of the time, and it was clear he was caught in a cycle that was leading to serious health problems at best. I left him, reluctantly, and while in another town considered suicide. I opened a bottle of sleeping pills thinking that if I died my husband could get on with his work without the pressure of my feelings, and my daughters certainly would not miss me. But something stopped me and I cried out, "No, it will not come to that!" What I did not know until later was that intercessors had been praying for me during that time! I found out when my husband came to visit me. We are now back together, living here near our daughters who have accepted me lovingly, and Bill is working a much lighter schedule.

God has shown me painfully yet gently that I am His child. My tears and prayers have led to an understanding I lacked before.

3. Compulsive Gambler

Those that sow in tears, shall reap in joy! What promises God has given me! My wife was a compulsive gambler for seventeen years—I kept asking for prayer for about a year and praise God the chains have been broken. I now have my wife back and our home is happy!

4. For a Good Job

I asked last year for prayer. We had no home, no job and had just lost a baby through miscarriage. On the last day of the three-week prayer period designated for us, my husband was offered a good job and I was suspicious that I was again pregnant. We now have a beautiful baby girl. Also, by the end of the three-week prayer period, we heard of a home to rent. It turned out to be more blessing than we could have dreamed, as we were able to buy the house last month. It took a full year for all this to happen, but last year we were "empty" and this year we are "full!"

5. A Cluttered Home

Catherine Marshall wrote in one of her books that once you lay everything in the Lord's hands, you sometimes get a shaking up. That happened to us. I have never been able to break the bad habit of keeping a cluttered house. Finally I prayed about it and put it into the Lord's hands. We had a very bad chimney fire which, fortunately, was confined to the chimney and no one was hurt, but the smoke damage was terrible. Our insurance adjuster sent out a team of professional housecleaners to clean up the mess and the results are so beautiful I now feel able to keep it uncluttered!

6. Fear of AIDS

It was one of the hardest times of my life—I could hardly pray for myself and so the prayers of others were like a gift. I am a nurse and was fearful of working with the many AIDS patients that were coming in. During my prayer period, I began to feel I could handle the situation and am now confident I will manage calmly. As I review my life, I can see that God's pattern for me has not necessarily been to take my problems away but rather to give me good examples and good resources to cope with the difficult situations.

7. Serious Auto Accident

I had asked prayer for healing of a young mother who had suffered head injuries in an automobile accident in which her husband was killed. The doctors advised her family to place her in a nursing home since her coma was so deep. They had little hope of her recovery. Shortly after I requested prayer she began to show signs of waking up. One afternoon she turned to her mother and spoke to her and has been awake ever since. Though she will need therapy for some time, there is no memory loss, no paralysis and she has been home to visit her ten-month-old daughter.

8. Cancer in a Two-Year-Old

I wanted to let you know that it appears that the two-year-old girl I asked prayer for with neuroblastoma is healed. The chemotherapy eliminated her secondary tumors and surgery found not a dead primary tumor as expected, but benign cells. I understand this has never happened before in a child over the age of one!

9. A Child Under Water Fifteen Minutes

I requested prayer for a baby who fell into a well and was submerged in water for fifteen minutes. The doctors gave little hope, saying that if the child lived there would be brain damage. Thank God, the child has recovered completely and is at home with his family. The doctors are saying his miraculous recovery has nothing to do with their skills and attribute it to a "higher power" as they put it. I give the glory to God.

10. To Have a Baby

We had been asking prayer for our friends who were unable to have a baby and had been waiting six years. I wrote a little while ago to tell you that although they were not yet expecting one, the Lord had answered this young couple's needs by helping them get financially organized, becoming more stable and disciplined and leading them to an appropriate medical group where they felt confident their fertility problems could be overcome. Now, however, I am excited and blessed to report that they will become parents in March.

11. Intercession in Church

In the two years since I became an intercessor, my family and I have been blessed because of your intercessors' love and prayers. My prayer journey has let me walk with 30 people in 21 states and one foreign country. Because of my walk of intercession with Breakthrough, I went to my church asking that we incorporate prayer along the same lines. The result is that we have received over 1,000 prayer requests and 100 praise reports. God bless this wonderful ongoing vision of Catherine Marshall.

12. Building Faith

Your prayer ministry builds faith. Often when I receive the prayer requests of others, there has been sickness or trouble in my own family. I don't believe I would have spent as much time in prayer for those problems of our own household if I hadn't been praying for others. These strangers I am praying for have become a part of my life and are in and out of my thoughts day and night.

Summary

Is there a central element that knits these twelve prayer requests together?

Yes—*unselfish prayer.*

When people pray for other people, something dynamic happens. The selfless quality of these pleas touches the heart of God. We feel that unselfish prayer moves God into action when perhaps nothing else would. He loves to see this kind of spiritual maturity in His children.

God has a special love for intercessors. That's why He is calling so many of us into this work.

If you are one of these, you will be blessed.

Hodder Christian Paperbacks: a tradition of excellence.

Great names and great books to enrich your life and meet your needs. Choose from such authors as:

Corrie ten Boom	Jackie Pullinger
Charles Colson	David Pytches
Richard Foster	Mary Pytches
Billy Graham	Jennifer Rees Larcombe
Michael Green	Cliff Richard
Michele Guinness	John Stott
Joyce Huggett	Joni Eareckson Tada
Francis MacNutt	Colin Urquhart
Catherine Marshall	David Watson
Jim Packer	David Wilkerson
Adrian Plass	John Wimber

The wide range of books on the Hodder Christian Paperback list include biography, personal testimony, devotional books, evangelistic books, Christian teaching, fiction, drama, poetry, books that give help for times of need – and many others.

Ask at your nearest Christian bookshop or at your church bookstall for the latest titles.

SOME BESTSELLERS IN
HODDER CHRISTIAN PAPERBACK

The Hiding Place – Corrie ten Boom

The triumphant story of Corrie ten Boom, heroine of the anti-Nazi underground.

"A brave and heartening story."   *Baptist Times*

God's Smuggler – Brother Andrew

An international bestseller. God's Smuggler carries contraband Bibles past armed border guards to bring the love of Christ to the people behind the Iron Curtain.

"A book you will not want to miss." *Catherine Marshall*

Discipleship – David Watson

"... breath-taking, block-busting, Bible-based simplicity on every page."   *Jim Packer*

Listening to God – Joyce Huggett

A profound spiritual testimony, and practical help for discovering a new dimension of prayer.

"This is counselling at its best."   *Leadership Today*

Celebration of Discipline – Richard Foster

A classic on the Spiritual Disciplines.

"For any Christian hungry for teaching, I would recommend this as being one of the most challenging books to have been published." *Delia Smith*

Run Baby Run – Nicky Cruz with Jamie Buckingham

A tough New York gang leader discovers Christ.

"It is a thrilling story. My hope is that it shall have a wide reading." *Billy Graham*

Chasing the Dragon – Jackie Pullinger with Andrew Quicke

Life-changing miracles in Hong Kong's Walled City.

"A book to stop you in your tracks."
Liverpool Daily Post

Born Again – Charles Colson

Disgraced by Watergate, Charles Colson finds a new life.

"An action packed story of real life drama and a revelation of modern history as well as a moving personal account." *Elim Evangel*

Knowing God – J I Packer

The biblical portrait that has become a classic.

"(The author) illumines every doctrine he touches and commends it with courage, logic, lucidity and warmth . . . the truth he handles fires the heart. At least it fired mine, and compelled me to turn aside to worship and pray." *John Stott*

The Happiest People on Earth – Demos Shakarian with John and Elizabeth Sherrill

The extraordinary beginnings of the Full Gospel Business Men's Fellowship.